SMOKIN' & GRILLIN'

WITH AARON BROWN

SMOKIN' & GRILLIN'

WITH AARON BROWN

More Than 100 Spectacular Recipes
FOR COOKING OUTDOORS

AARON BROWN

HARVARD
COMMON
PRESS

Quarto.com

© 2024 Quarto Publishing Group USA Inc.
Text © 2024 Smokin' & Grillin' Wit AB LLC

First Published in 2024 by The Harvard Common Press, an imprint of The Quarto Group,
100 Cummings Center, Suite 265-D, Beverly, MA 01915, USA.
T (978) 282-9590 F (978) 283-2742

The Harvard Common Press titles are also available at discount for retail, wholesale, promotional, and bulk purchase. For details, con-tact the Special Sales Manager by email at specialsales@quarto.com or by mail at The Quarto Group, Attn: Special Sales Manager, 100 Cummings Center, Suite 265-D, Beverly, MA 01915, USA.

28 27 26 25 24   1 2 3 4 5

ISBN: 978-0-7603-8918-8

Digital edition published in 2024
eISBN: 978-0-7603-8919-5

Library of Congress Cataloging-in-Publication Data

Names: Brown, Aaron (Writer on cooking), author.
Title: Smokin' and grillin' with Aaron Brown : more than 100 spectacular
   recipes for cooking outdoors / Aaron Brown.
Description: Beverly, MA, USA : Harvard Common Press, 2024. | Includes
   index. | Summary: "YouTube's guru of grilling reveals his brilliant-and
   delectable-secrets, and takes your BBQ game up several notches, in
   Smokin' and Grillin' with Aaron Brown"-- Provided by publisher.
Identifiers: LCCN 2023056293 (print) | LCCN 2023056294 (ebook)
| ISBN
   9780760389188 (hardcover) | ISBN 9780760389195 (ebook)
Subjects: LCSH: Barbecuing. | Outdoor cooking. | Smoking (Cooking)
| LCGFT:
   Cookbooks.
Classification: LCC TX840.B3 B7575 2024 (print) | LCC TX840.B3
(ebook) |
   DDC 641.5/784--dc23/eng/20231206
LC record available at https://lccn.loc.gov/2023056293
LC ebook record available at https://lccn.loc.gov/2023056294

Design and Page Layout: Kelley Galbreath
Front Cover Image: Jeffrey Green Photography
Back Cover Images: Zack Bowen Photography with styling by Catrine Kelty
Recipe Photography: Zack Bowen Photography
Recipe Styling and Propping: Catrine Kelty
Author Photography: Jeffrey Green Photography on pages 2, 8, 10 (right), 11 (right), 49, 51, 63, 72, 97, 116, 175, 179, 193, 194, and 197

Printed in China

This cookbook is a heartfelt tribute to my late grandfather, whose mastery of BBQ ignited my passion for grilling and smoking meats. His lessons, both in cooking and life, are the essence of these pages.

To my dear late mother, grandmother, and great-grandmother, your culinary wisdom forms the heart of this book. Your legacy lives on through the flavors and traditions you instilled in me.

With gratitude to those who shaped my love for cooking, and to all joining me on this flavorful journey, thank you for savoring the joy of BBQ and Southern flavors with me.

Savoring memories and flavors,
Aaron Brown (AB)

Contents

INTRODUCTION

Thanks for droppin' in!

WELCOME TO MY WORLD OF OUTDOOR COOKING! I'm AB, the chef behind *Smokin' and Grillin' with AB*.

Smokin' and Grillin' with AB is what I call my online channel—on YouTube and some other online places—where I share cooking videos and lots of outdoor cooking wisdom I've picked up over many years of good times grillin' and smokin'. I am very grateful for the millions of people who have watched my videos and left notes of appreciation in the comments sections.

But there is one thing I have never done, and that is to write out and share my best grilling and smoking recipes. Not online, not in a book. Now I have, right here in these pages. I hope you'll enjoy having them. I know a lot of you have been asking for them.

In this cookbook, I ain't just sharing recipes; I want you to experience the joy of cooking in the great outdoors. From tender marinated meats to smoky grilled veggies, each page and recipe reflect my passion for outdoor cooking and the genuine delight I find in sharing it with others.

For me, the grill is more than just a cooking tool; it's a source of happiness and a way to create cherished memories with family and friends. Whether you're having a laid-back backyard gathering with family or an exciting cookout for a crowd, I hope my cookbook will be your guide to crafting delicious masterpieces and creating unforgettable moments. From timeless BBQ classics to new favorites, I'll be your neighbor, as if we were cooking together in my own backyard.

But this cookbook isn't just about food; it's also about the camaraderie around the grill. I believe that grilling, smoking, and preparing food outdoors is meant to be shared, and I encourage you all to infuse each recipe with your own flair and creativity.

As we dive deep into the world of grillin' and smokin', I will be sharing my best-kept secrets. Along the way, I'll be sharing with you all stories, laughter, and heartfelt memories, some of which will echo your own memories of your gatherings and journey. So, grab your apron and fire up the coals. Let this cookbook be your guide as we create unforgettable recipes!

A word about the kinds of recipes you will find in this book: About two-thirds are for grilling, one-third for smoking. Some recipes are for "grill-roasting" on a grill (as opposed to a dedicated smoker), and these recipes are in between grilling and smoking. Because most people own a grill but not everyone has a smoker, I thought this two-thirds to one-third ratio was just about right. Note that you *can* smoke-cook pretty successfully on a covered grill. The recipe on page 71 shows how. If you have a covered grill but not a smoker, follow the method used in that recipe to do some smokin' on your grill, for any of the other smoking recipes in this book.

Don't forget, it's more than just cooking; it's also about embracing the outdoors, enjoying life's simple pleasures, and cherishing the moments with loved ones.

Let's get it!

CHAPTER

One

CHICKEN & TURKEY

THE AB WAY

FROM THE

Grill

Mediterranean
GRILLED STUFFED CHICKEN BREAST

SERVES 4

PREP TIME: 25 minutes
COOK TIME: 34 minutes

1 teaspoon olive oil
2 cups (60 g) spinach leaves
8 ounces (227 g) soft goat cheese, at room temperature
¼ cup (40 g) chopped oil-marinated sun-dried tomatoes
4 boneless, skinless chicken breasts
2 tablespoons (12 g) poultry seasoning

YOU COULD SERVE ME A MIXTURE of goat cheese, sun-dried tomatoes, and spinach straight up and I would not complain. But if you stuff it into some chicken breasts and toss them on the grill, well, I'll be your friend forever. This one's fancy enough for company on the weekend but quick and easy enough for supper on a busy weeknight.

1 Preheat the grill to medium-high heat using half the burners on one side (leaving the other burners off), about 400°F (200°C).

2 Heat the oil in a medium skillet over medium heat. Add the spinach and toss using tongs until wilted, about 2 minutes.

3 Transfer the spinach to a medium bowl and add the goat cheese and sun-dried tomatoes, stirring until very well combined.

4 Cut the chicken breasts through the middle lengthwise to create a pocket, but don't cut all the way through! Evenly divide the filling among the breasts, stuffing it into the pocket, and secure the edges of the breast with toothpicks to seal the filling in. Season the chicken with poultry seasoning.

5 Place the chicken breasts on the hot side of the grill and grill until lightly browned, turning halfway through, about 12 minutes in total. Transfer the chicken to the cooler side, close the grill lid, and cook until the chicken has an internal temperature of 165°F (74°C), about 20 minutes.

6 Remove the toothpicks and serve.

Bang Bang CHICKEN SKEWERS

SERVES 4

PREP TIME: *25 minutes*
COOK TIME: *12 minutes*

For the Skewers
2 pounds (910 g) boneless, skinless
   chicken breasts, cut into 1-inch
   (2.5 cm) cubes
1 tablespoon (15 ml) olive oil
1 ½ teaspoons smoked paprika
1 teaspoon garlic powder
½ teaspoon salt
¼ teaspoon freshly ground black
   pepper
8 metal skewers or wooden
   skewers soaked in water for
   30 minutes

For the Bang Bang Sauce
1 cup (240 ml) mayonnaise
¾ cup (180 ml) sweet chili sauce
2 tablespoons (40 g) honey
1 tablespoon (15 ml) sriracha sauce

BANG BANG SAUCE, ALSO KNOWN AS bam bam or bon bon sauce, is the quintessential street food sauce in China. Take it from the street to the backyard grill and it's still a winner. I use it on chicken dishes but it's also unbeatable on shrimp especially, as well as on any other fish or shellfish you want to grill.

1 Preheat the grill to medium-high heat, about 400°F (200°C).

2 To make the skewers, in a large bowl, toss the chicken, oil, paprika, garlic powder, salt, and pepper until well mixed. Thread the chicken onto 8 skewers, leaving a bit of space to allow for even cooking.

3 Grill the skewers for 20 minutes, turning often, until cooked through, 165°F (74°C) internal temperature, and lightly charred.

4 To make the sauce, while the chicken is grilling, in a small bowl, mix the mayonnaise, chili sauce, honey, and sriracha. Serve with the skewers.

Teriyaki-Glazed
CHICKEN & PINEAPPLE GRILLED KABOBS

SERVES 4

PREP TIME: *20 minutes,*
plus marinating time
COOK TIME: *22 minutes*

½ cup (120 ml) teriyaki sauce
½ cup (120 ml) barbecue sauce
1 tablespoon (8 g) minced garlic
1 tablespoon (8 g) peeled and
    grated fresh ginger
2 pounds (910 g) boneless,
    skinless chicken breasts, cut
    into 1-inch (2.5 cm) chunks
2 cups (340 g) fresh pineapple
    chunks
2 red bell peppers, seeded and cut
    into 1 ½-inch (3.8 cm) pieces
8 metal skewers or wooden
    skewers soaked in water for
    30 minutes

PINEAPPLE IS THE FRUIT that takes best to the grill, although many other fruits, such as peaches and watermelon, grill up nicely. The sweet-and-hot teriyaki glaze makes these kabobs explode with flavor.

1   In a medium bowl, whisk together the teriyaki sauce, barbecue sauce, garlic, and ginger until well combined. Reserve ½ cup (120 ml) of the mixture.

2   Add the chicken to the bowl, tossing to coat, cover, and refrigerate for at least 2 hours and up to 8 hours.

3   Thread the chicken, pineapple, and red pepper onto 8 skewers, leaving a bit of space to allow for even cooking. Discard the sauce in the bowl.

4   Preheat the grill to medium heat, about 350°F (180°C). Grill the skewers for 20 minutes, turning often, until cooked through and lightly charred. Brush the skewers with the reserved sauce and grill for 2 minutes. Serve.

Buffalo Maple
CHICKEN THIGHS

SERVES 6

PREP TIME: *15 minutes*
COOK TIME: *30 minutes*

½ cup (120 ml) hot sauce
(like Frank's)
3 tablespoons (45 ml)
maple syrup
2 teaspoons minced garlic
2 pounds (910 g) boneless, skinless
chicken thighs
Salt and freshly ground black
pepper
1 scallion, white and green parts,
finely chopped

I'VE ALWAYS LOVED THE "mostly white meat with a hint of dark meat" character of chicken thighs, not to mention the fact that they cook up quick and easy on the grill. Adjust the hot sauce quantity here to your liking, keeping in mind that you'll lose that Buffalo-style flavor if you cut the hot sauce down too low.

1 Preheat the grill to medium heat, about 350°F (180°C), and lightly oil the grates.

2 In a small bowl, combine the hot sauce, maple syrup, and garlic.

3 Season the chicken with salt and pepper in a medium bowl. Add 3 tablespoons (45 ml) of the sauce and toss to coat the chicken.

4 Grill the chicken, flipping the thighs every 4 minutes, until they reach an internal temperature of 165°F (74°C), about 30 minutes total. During the last 12 minutes of grilling, brush the thighs with the sauce before flipping them.

5 Serve topped with the scallions.

Grilled
CHICKEN THIGHS

SERVES 3

PREP TIME: 10 minutes, plus marinating time
COOK TIME: 30 minutes

½ teaspoon garlic powder
½ teaspoon onion powder
½ teaspoon smoked paprika
½ teaspoon kosher salt
¼ teaspoon freshly ground black pepper
6 bone-in chicken thighs
½ cup (120 ml) your favorite barbecue sauce

THERE ARE A MILLION SPICE MIXTURES and rubs in the world of grilling and smoking. If I had to name the Mother of All Spice Mixtures, this combination of garlic and onion powders, plus smoked paprika, salt, and pepper, would be it. It's not the best for fish, but it will serve you well with any other kind of meat.

1 Add the garlic powder, onion powder, paprika, salt, and pepper to a large resealable plastic bag and shake to combine.

2 Add the chicken thighs to the bag, shaking to coat them, and squeeze out as much air as possible, seal, and refrigerate for 2 hours.

3 Preheat the grill to medium heat, about 350°F (180°C), and lightly oil the grates.

4 Grill the chicken skin-side down for 8 minutes, turn them, and grill for 4 minutes. Brush the thighs with barbecue sauce, flip them, and cook 4 minutes, and then brush the sauce on again. Cook, brush, and flip until the thighs are cooked through with an internal temperature of 165°F (74°C). The total grilling time is about 30 minutes. Serve.

Bourbon Maple
BBQ CHICKEN SKEWERS

SERVES 4

PREP TIME: 30 minutes
COOK TIME: 25 minutes

¾ cup (180 ml) ketchup
½ cup (120 ml) bourbon
2 tablespoons (30 ml) maple syrup
⅓ cup (65 g) packed brown sugar
1 tablespoon (15 ml) grainy mustard
1 tablespoon (15 ml) Worcestershire sauce
2 teaspoons chili powder
2 teaspoons smoked paprika
1 teaspoon garlic powder
Salt and freshly ground black pepper
2 pounds (910 g) boneless, skinless chicken thighs, cut into 2-inch (5 cm) chunks
8 metal skewers or wooden skewers soaked in water for 30 minutes

THERE IS A NATURAL SWEETNESS TO BOURBON, not to mention a smoky flavor and aroma. Both of those things make it a sure bet when you are concocting your own homemade marinades and sauces for grilling or smoking. Here's one of my sauces (divided into two batches, a basting or mopping sauce and a table or finishing sauce) that turns grilled chicken into something special.

1 Preheat the grill to medium heat, about 350°F (180°C).

2 In a medium saucepan, whisk together the ketchup, bourbon, maple syrup, brown sugar, mustard, Worcestershire sauce, chili powder, paprika, and garlic powder and bring to a boil over medium heat. Reduce the heat to low and simmer, whisking occasionally, for 10 minutes. Season to taste with salt and pepper. Let the sauce cool for 15 minutes.

3 Season the chicken with salt and pepper.

4 Reserve ½ cup (120 ml) of sauce and pour the rest into a medium bowl. Add the chicken and toss to combine. Thread the chicken onto 8 skewers, leaving a bit of space to allow for even cooking. Discard the sauce in the bowl.

5 Grill the chicken for 15 minutes, turning often, until cooked through with an internal temperature of 165°F (74°C) and lightly charred.

6 Serve the skewers with the reserved barbecue sauce.

Jamaican Jerk
CHICKEN WINGS

SERVES 4

PREP TIME: 10 minutes, plus marinating time
COOK TIME: 40 minutes

½ cup (120 ml) olive oil
Juice of ½ orange
Juice of 2 limes
½ cup (80 g) finely chopped onion
1 jalapeño pepper, seeded and minced
2 tablespoons (25 g) packed brown sugar
1 tablespoon (8 g) minced garlic
2 teaspoons peeled and grated fresh ginger
2 teaspoons freshly ground black pepper
2 teaspoons dried thyme
1 teaspoon smoked paprika
1 teaspoon ground allspice
1 teaspoon kosher salt
1 teaspoon ground nutmeg
½ teaspoon ground cinnamon
½ teaspoon cayenne pepper
4 pounds (1.8 kg) chicken wings

I STAND BY THIS VERSION of jerk wings over the dozens of others that are out there. After lots of trial and error, this is the blend of spices that hits the right notes for me. I've served these wings at lots of gatherings of family and friends and I can tell you with confidence that everybody loves 'em.

1 Place the oil, orange juice, lime juice, onion, jalapeño, brown sugar, garlic, ginger, black pepper, thyme, paprika, allspice, salt, nutmeg, cinnamon, and cayenne in a large resealable plastic bag and shake to combine.

2 Add the chicken wings, squeeze out as much air as possible, and seal the bag. Massage the marinade into the wings and refrigerate for at least 2 hours and up to overnight.

3 Preheat the grill to medium-high heat, about 400°F (200°C).

4 Place the chicken wings on the grill and discard the marinade. Grill, turning every 10 minutes, until the chicken skin is crispy and golden and the wings have an internal temperature of 165°F (74°C), about 40 minutes. Serve.

Teriyaki
GRILLED CHICKEN DRUMSTICKS

SERVES 4

PREP TIME: *10 minutes, plus marinating time*
COOK TIME: *40 minutes*

1 cup (240 ml) water
¼ cup (60 ml) low-sodium soy sauce
¼ cup (50 g) brown sugar
2 tablespoons (16 g) peeled and grated fresh ginger
1 tablespoon (8 g) minced garlic
2 tablespoons (16 g) cornstarch
8 chicken drumsticks

NOBODY—AS FAR AS I KNOW—makes tempura on the grill. But the cornstarch in this teriyaki-style sauce makes for a crisp coating that will remind you of a tempura dish. This is one of my most popular things to make when I cook for a crowd. Kids like these, too.

1 In a medium saucepan, whisk together ¾ cup (180 ml) of the water, soy sauce, brown sugar, ginger, and garlic and bring to a boil over medium heat.

2 In a small bowl, stir together the remaining ¼ cup (60 ml) of water and cornstarch until blended. Pour the cornstarch mixture into the saucepan and whisk continuously until the sauce thickens, about 2 minutes. Remove the saucepan from the heat and let the sauce cool to room temperature.

3 Pour ½ cup (120 ml) of the sauce into a large resealable plastic bag and add the drumsticks. Press out as much air as possible, seal the bag, shake it a few times, and refrigerate for 2 hours. Reserve the remaining sauce.

4 Preheat the grill to medium heat, about 350°F (180°C).

5 Arrange the drumsticks on the grill, basting with the reserved sauce. Grill the chicken for 10 minutes, turn them, and baste them again. Continue grilling, turning, and basting every 10 minutes until the chicken is cooked through with an internal temperature of 165°F (74°C), about 30 minutes longer. Serve.

BUFFALO CHICKEN
Lollipops

SERVES 4

PREP TIME: 20 minutes, plus marinating time
COOK TIME: 30 minutes

12 chicken drumsticks
1 teaspoon smoked paprika
½ teaspoon garlic powder
¾ cup (180 ml) hot sauce (like Frank's)
½ cup (112 g) unsalted butter, melted

YOU WOULD THINK THAT A DISH with a funny name like this would have one, maybe two versions out in the world. Nope. There are dozens and dozens. I can't claim that this simple one is 100 percent unique. But I can guarantee you that grilling makes these popular drumsticks taste better than any oven or stovetop rendition. Give 'em a shot.

1 Score around the bone of the drumsticks about 2 inches (5 cm) from the knuckle. Push the meat down the drumstick to expose the bone and trim off the excess skin.

2 Season the drumsticks with the paprika and garlic powder and refrigerate them (covered) for at least 2 hours and up to 8 hours.

3 Preheat the grill to medium heat, about 350°F (180°C), and oil the grates.

4 Sear the lollipops, turning to get all sides, for 10 minutes. Continue to grill, turning, until the chicken is thoroughly cooked through with an internal temperature 165°F (74°C), about 20 minutes.

5 In a large bowl, whisk together the hot sauce and butter until smooth and add the cooked lollipops. Toss to coat them and serve.

GRILLED CHICKEN
with Lemon & Herbs

SERVES 6

PREP TIME: 15 minutes, plus marinating time
COOK TIME: 15 minutes

½ cup (120 ml) olive oil
Juice of 2 lemons
3 tablespoons (12 g) chopped fresh parsley, plus more for garnish
2 tablespoons (8 g) chopped fresh basil
1 tablespoon (4 g) chopped fresh mint
2 teaspoons minced garlic
½ teaspoon kosher salt
¼ teaspoon freshly ground black pepper
1 ½ pounds (680 g) boneless, skinless chicken breasts, pounded to 1 inch (2.5 cm) thick
1 lemon, cut into wedges

JUDGING BY HOW MUCH SPACE they take up in supermarket meat departments, boneless, skinless chicken breasts are nowadays the most popular cut of meat among home cooks. I've cooked them dozens of ways on the grill, and this straightforward recipe never fails to please. Play with the herb mixture if this one doesn't suit your taste; thyme and oregano, for example, are other time-tested herbs for chicken.

1 Add the olive oil, lemon juice, parsley, basil, mint, garlic, salt, and pepper to a large resealable plastic bag and shake to combine.

2 Add the chicken breasts to the bag, squeeze out as much air as possible, seal, and massage the marinade into the chicken. Refrigerate for at least 1 hour and up to 8 hours.

3 Preheat the grill to medium heat, about 350°F (180°C), and lightly oil the grates.

4 Grill the chicken until it is lightly charred and cooked through with an internal temperature of 165°F (74°C), turning once, about 15 minutes in total.

5 Remove the chicken to a platter, tent it loosely with foil, and let it rest for 5 minutes. Squeeze the lemon wedges over the chicken, garnish with parsley, and serve.

Maple Rosemary
GRILLED CHICKEN

SERVES 4

PREP TIME: 15 minutes, plus marinating time
COOK TIME: 20 minutes

½ cup (120 ml) maple syrup
3 tablespoons (45 ml) olive oil
3 tablespoons (45 ml) soy sauce
2 tablespoons (8 g) chopped fresh rosemary
1 tablespoon (15 ml) Dijon mustard
1 tablespoon (8 g) minced garlic
Six 5-ounce (140 g) boneless, skinless chicken breasts

OF ALL THE HERBS, the one that I think goes together best in a marinade with maple syrup is rosemary. There is a sort of fall and winter holiday festiveness in the flavor combination, but you can cook this tangy, herby, sweet chicken dish any time of year, as far as I'm concerned.

1 Add the maple syrup, olive oil, soy sauce, rosemary, mustard, and garlic to a large resealable plastic bag and shake to combine.

2 Add the chicken breasts to the bag, shaking to coat them, squeeze out as much air as possible, seal, and refrigerate for 1 hour and up to overnight.

3 Preheat the grill to medium heat, about 350°F (180°C), and lightly oil the grates.

4 Grill the chicken, turning occasionally, until golden and with an internal temperature of 165°F (74°C), about 20 minutes. Serve.

Spatchcock
CHICKEN ON THE GRILL

SERVES 4

PREP TIME: 20 minutes
COOK TIME: 50 minutes

1 teaspoon smoked paprika
½ teaspoon dried oregano
½ teaspoon garlic powder
½ teaspoon salt
¼ teaspoon freshly ground black pepper
1 tablespoon (15 ml) olive oil
One 4-pound (1.8 kg) whole chicken, backbone removed with kitchen shears and pressed flat

THIS IS HANDS-DOWN MY GO-TO WAY to grill a whole chicken. The spatchcocking method has two big advantages. One, it really lets the whole bird get the flavors of the spices, because there are no hidden surfaces. Two, it exposes more of the bird to the heat of the grill, meaning it takes less time to cook (and cooks more evenly) than a regular whole chicken would.

1 Preheat the grill to medium heat, about 350°F (180°C), and place a drip pan under the grates.

2 In a small bowl, combine the paprika, oregano, garlic powder, salt, and pepper.

3 Rub the olive oil on the chicken and season it all over with the spice and herb mixture.

4 Place the chicken breast-side down over the drip pan and grill for 10 minutes. Flip the chicken over and grill until it reaches an internal temperature of 165°F (74°C), about 40 minutes longer.

5 Remove the chicken to a platter, tent it loosely with foil, and let it rest for 10 minutes before carving it.

Sweet Tea-Marinated GRILLED CHICKEN

SERVES 4

PREP TIME: 15 minutes, plus 24 hours marinating time
COOK TIME: 30 minutes

4 cups (960 ml) water
2 tea bags (English breakfast, orange pekoe, or oolong)
½ cup (100 g) sugar
1 tablespoon (17 g) salt
1 lemon, thinly sliced
3 cloves garlic, smashed
4 thyme sprigs
½ teaspoon black peppercorns
One 4-pound (1.8 kg) whole chicken, cut into pieces
Lemon wedges or slices, for garnish

FOLKS HAVE BEEN DRINKING SWEET TEA and eating grilled chicken in the South for generations. But it was only in recent years, influenced, perhaps, by the use of tea in some Asian cooking, that the two traditions got together in one dish. The results are really delicious.

1 Bring the water to a boil in a kettle and pour it into a large bowl. Add the tea bags and steep for 10 minutes. Squeeze out the bags and discard them.

2 Add the sugar, salt, lemon slices, garlic, thyme, and peppercorns to the tea and let it cool to room temperature.

3 Add the chicken pieces, cover, and refrigerate for 24 hours.

4 Preheat the grill to medium heat, about 350°F (180°C).

5 Place the chicken on the grill skin-side down, close the lid, and grill, flipping every 10 minutes, until the chicken is golden with an internal temperature of 165°F (74°C), about 30 minutes total time. Garnish with lemon wedges or slices.

Bacon-Wrapped
JALAPEÑO POPPER STUFFED CHICKEN

SERVES 4

PREP TIME: 25 minutes
COOK TIME: 30 minutes

¼ cup (60 g) cream cheese, at room temperature

¼ cup (40 g) finely shredded sharp Cheddar cheese

2 tablespoons (16 g) minced jalapeño pepper

Four 5-ounce (140 g) chicken breasts, pounded to ½ inch (1.3 cm) thick

Salt and freshly ground black pepper

8 slices bacon

SOME FOLKS WILL WRAP BACON around just about anything. I'm a little more particular. This is an intensely flavorful way to dress up some chicken breasts for an easy feast.

1 Preheat the grill to medium heat, about 350°F (180°C), using half the burners on one side (leaving the other burners off).

2 In a small bowl, beat the cream cheese, Cheddar, and jalapeño until very well combined and almost smooth.

3 Lay the chicken breasts flat on a piece of parchment paper and season with salt and pepper. Evenly divide the filling among the breasts, spreading it to the edges. Roll the breasts up firmly and wrap each with 2 slices of bacon, overlapping the edges and tucking in the ends.

4 Place the wrapped chicken rolls on the cooler side of the grill, close the grill lid, and cook, turning occasionally, until the bacon is crispy and the chicken is cooked through with an internal temperature of 165°F (74°C), about 30 minutes. Serve.

GRILLED CHICKEN SANDWICH
with Honey BBQ Sauce

SERVES 4

PREP TIME: *15 minutes*
COOK TIME: *45 minutes*

1 teaspoon olive oil

½ sweet onion, finely chopped

1 tablespoon (8 g) minced garlic

¾ cup (180 ml) water

One 6-ounce (168 g) can tomato
   paste

¼ cup (80 g) honey

2 tablespoons (30 ml) apple cider
   vinegar

1 tablespoon (6 g) chili powder

2 teaspoons celery seeds

1 teaspoon smoked paprika

Salt and freshly ground black
   pepper

Four 6-ounce (168 g) boneless,
   skinless chicken breasts

4 hamburger buns or kaiser
   rolls, toasted

Sliced tomatoes, for topping

Pickle slices, for topping

Lettuce, for topping

YOU CAN BUY A HONEYED BARBECUE SAUCE easily nowadays, but it won't be as good as the homemade version in this recipe. Make some extra if you like, and store it, covered, in the refrigerator for up to a week.

1   Preheat the grill to medium heat, about 350°F (180°C), and oil the grates.

2   In a medium saucepan, heat the oil over medium-high heat. Add the onion and garlic and sauté until softened, about 3 minutes. Stir in the water, tomato paste, honey, apple cider vinegar, chili powder, celery seeds, and smoked paprika. Bring the sauce to a boil, reduce the heat to low, cover, and simmer until thickened, about 20 minutes. Season with salt and pepper.

3   Grill the chicken breasts, turning and brushing with the honey barbecue sauce, until cooked through with an internal temperature of 165°F (74°C), 15 to 18 minutes total.

4   Slather about 1 tablespoon (15 ml) of sauce onto each bun and top the bottom buns with a chicken breast, tomato, pickles, and lettuce. Add the top buns and serve.

Summertime
GRILLED CHICKEN SALAD

SERVES 4

PREP TIME: *30 minutes, plus marinating time*
COOK TIME: *30 minutes*

¼ cup (60 ml) olive oil
¼ cup (16 g) chopped fresh parsley
2 tablespoons (12 g) paprika
2 teaspoons minced garlic
1 teaspoon salt
½ teaspoon freshly ground black pepper
1 ½ pounds (680 g) boneless, skinless chicken thighs
8 cups (240 g) baby mixed greens
1 English cucumber, chopped
2 cups (300 g) halved cherry tomatoes
1 yellow bell pepper, seeded and chopped
½ small red onion, thinly sliced
½ cup (60 g) crumbled feta cheese
Your favorite salad dressing

LET'S TALK ABOUT A DISH that's all about freshness and flavor: the grilled chicken salad. One day as my chicken was cooking on the grill, I chopped up some crisp lettuce, tomatoes, cucumber, and red onion. I tossed it all together, and there it was: a chicken salad that looked and tasted like summer. It's a welcome departure from the same ol', same ol' chicken salad you're used to.

1 Add the olive oil, parsley, paprika, garlic, salt, and pepper to a large resealable plastic bag and shake to combine.

2 Add the chicken thighs to the bag, shake to coat them, squeeze out as much air as possible, seal, and refrigerate for 1 hour.

3 Preheat the grill to medium heat, about 350°F (180°C), and lightly oil the grates.

4 Grill the chicken, turning every 8 minutes, until the thighs are cooked through with an internal temperature of 165°F (74°C). The total grilling time is about 30 minutes.

5 Remove the chicken from the grill and chop into bite-size pieces.

6 Arrange the greens, cucumber, cherry tomatoes, bell pepper, onion, and feta on four plates and top with the grilled chicken. Dress the salads and serve.

Grilled Chicken &
PARMESAN SOUP

SERVES 6 AS A FIRST COURSE, 4 AS A MAIN COURSE

PREP TIME: 20 minutes
COOK TIME: 26 minutes

1 pound (455 g) boneless, skinless chicken breasts
Italian seasoning
1 tablespoon (15 ml) olive oil
1 sweet onion, chopped
3 celery stalks, chopped
2 carrots, thinly sliced into rounds
1 tablespoon (8 g) minced garlic
4 cups (960 ml) chicken broth
One 14 ½-ounce (406 g) can diced tomatoes, undrained
One 6-ounce (168 g) can tomato paste
6 ounces (168 g) penne or rotini pasta
¾ cup (75 g) grated Parmesan cheese

A LOT OF CHICKEN SOUPS ARE MADE with boring boiled chicken. Some take a step up and use roasted chicken. But if you want a really robust and flavor-packed chicken soup, you can't do better than to make it with grilled chicken. Here's one soup that I make often, but there's really no chicken soup that isn't better when it's made with chicken hot from the grill.

1 Preheat the grill to medium-high heat, about 400°F (200°C). Clean and coat the grates with nonstick cooking spray.

2 Season the chicken with Italian seasoning. Grill the chicken, turning halfway through the cooking time, until cooked through with an internal temperature of 165°F (74°C), about 25 minutes. Transfer the chicken to a cutting board and dice it.

3 While the chicken is grilling, heat the oil in a large pot over medium-high heat. Add the onion, celery, and carrots and sauté until softened, about 6 minutes. Add the garlic and sauté for 2 minutes longer.

4 Add the chicken broth, diced tomatoes with juices, and tomato paste and bring to a boil. Stir in the pasta and cook, stirring occasionally, until the pasta is tender, about 18 minutes.

5 Add the diced chicken and Parmesan cheese and serve immediately.

Grill-Smoked CHICKEN & SAUSAGE GUMBO

SERVES 8

PREP TIME: *20 minutes*
COOK TIME: *1 ½ hours*

2 tablespoons (30 ml) and ½ cup (120 ml) vegetable oil
One 3-pound (1,365 g) whole chicken, giblets removed
Salt and freshly ground black pepper
1 pound (455 g) smoked andouille sausage, cut into ¼-inch (6 mm) slices
½ cup (60 g) all-purpose flour
4 celery stalks, chopped
2 red bell peppers, seeded and chopped
1 large onion, chopped
8 to 10 fresh okra pods, stemmed and sliced lengthwise
2 teaspoons minced garlic
2 quarts (1.8 L) chicken broth
2 bay leaves
2 tablespoons (12 g) Creole seasoning
Chopped fresh parsley, for garnish
Cooked white rice, for serving

THE DIRECTIONS FOR SMOKING the chicken in this recipe are for indirect heat smoking on a regular grill, which is a nice technique to learn if you do not own a dedicated smoker. If on the other hand you do own a smoker, you can smoke the chicken using the same time and temperature guidance you see below.

1 Preheat the grill to medium-high heat, about 400°F (200°C), using half the burners on one side (leaving the other burners off). Place a drip pan on the cooler side.

2 Rub 1 tablespoon (15 ml) of the oil on the chicken and season it with salt and pepper. Place the chicken, breast-side up, in the center of the grill grate on the cool side. Wrap 2 or 3 hardwood chunks in foil and place them on the hot side of the grill. Roast until it is golden brown and cooked through with an internal temperature of 165°F (74°C), about 1 hour and 15 minutes. Transfer the chicken to a cutting board to cool.

3 While the chicken cooks, heat 1 tablespoon (15 ml) of oil in a large pot over medium-high heat. Add the sausage and cook until browned, about 6 minutes. Transfer the sausage to a paper towel–lined plate and set aside.

4 Combine the remaining ½ cup (120 ml) of oil and the flour in the pot over medium heat. Cook the roux, whisking constantly, until it is a dark, rich color, about 30 minutes.

5 Add the celery, bell peppers, onion, okra, and garlic and cook until softened, stirring frequently, about 6 minutes. Slowly pour in the chicken broth, stirring until the mixture is smooth. Add the bay leaves, Creole seasoning, and cooked sausage.

6 Bring the gumbo to a boil, reduce the heat to low, and simmer until thick, about 40 minutes.

7 Remove the meat from the chicken, chop it into bite-size pieces, and add it to the gumbo. Simmer for 10 minutes longer.

8 Remove the bay leaves and serve topped with chopped parsley over rice.

Grill-Roasted
BONELESS TURKEY BREAST, FOR HOLIDAYS OR EVERY DAY

SERVES 8

PREP TIME: *10 minutes*
COOK TIME: *2 hours*

1 teaspoon dried thyme
1 teaspoon dried sage
½ teaspoon dried rosemary
½ teaspoon salt
¼ teaspoon freshly ground black pepper
1 tablespoon (15 ml) olive oil
One 4-pound (1.8 kg) boneless, skin-on turkey breast
Fresh sage, for garnish
Lemon slices, for garnish

HAVE YOU EVER BEEN TO A HOLIDAY MEAL where turkey is served and *literally everyone* wants the white meat? If that happens often with your family and friends, I've got news for you: It's time to throw in the towel and cook nothing but turkey breast. This grill-roasted preparation will make everyone happy.

1 Preheat the grill to medium heat, about 350°F (180°C), and place a drip pan under the grates.

2 In a small bowl, combine the thyme, sage, rosemary, salt, and pepper.

3 Rub the olive oil on the turkey breast and season it all over with the herb mixture. Place the turkey over the drip pan and grill, turning every 20 minutes, until the turkey reaches an internal temperature of 160°F (71°C), about 2 hours.

4 Remove the turkey to a platter, tent it loosely with foil, and let it rest for 20 minutes before carving it.

5 Serve with sprigs of fresh sage and lemon slices.

Grill-Roasted
HERBED TURKEY LEGS

SERVES 6

PREP TIME: *20 minutes, plus 24 hours brining time*
COOK TIME: *1 hour and 45 minutes*

2 quarts (1.8 L) water
2 tablespoons (34 g) salt
5 cloves garlic, crushed
4 bay leaves
4 turkey legs
¼ cup (56 g) unsalted butter, melted
3 tablespoons (45 ml) canola oil
1 small onion, roughly chopped
2 tablespoons (30 ml) soy sauce
1 teaspoon dried thyme
1 teaspoon dried rosemary
1 teaspoon dried oregano
½ teaspoon dried basil

I KNOW PEOPLE WHO GREW UP in cash-strapped households but still ate really well. Almost all of them were served turkey legs fairly often. Turkey legs are a wallet-friendly budget cut that has lots of potential if you flavor them just right.

1 In a large bowl, combine the water, salt, garlic, and bay leaves and stir until the salt dissolves. Add the turkey legs, cover, and brine in the refrigerator for 24 hours.

2 Take the turkey legs out of the brine and pat them dry using paper towels.

3 In a food processor, add the butter, oil, onion, soy sauce, thyme, rosemary, oregano, and basil and pulse until smooth. Transfer the mixture to a bowl and set aside.

4 Preheat the grill to medium heat, about 350°F (180°C).

5 Place a rack in a large roasting pan and arrange the turkey legs on the rack. Place the roasting pan on the grill, close the lid, and cook for 30 minutes, and then brush the legs with the butter mixture. Continue cooking with the lid closed, brushing every 20 minutes, until the legs reach an internal temperature of 165°F (74°C) and the juices run clear, about 1 hour and 45 minutes total.

FROM THE
Smoker

Smoked Brined
CHICKEN BREASTS

SERVES 4

PREP TIME: 15 minutes, plus brining time
COOK TIME: 1 ½ hours

2 quarts (1.8 L) hot water
¼ cup (68 g) salt
½ cup (100 g) sugar
1 large carrot, roughly chopped
1 medium onion, roughly chopped
4 cloves garlic, crushed
2 bay leaves
2 teaspoons black peppercorns
Four 6-ounce (168 g) bone-in, skin-on chicken breasts
1 tablespoon (15 ml) olive oil
3 tablespoons (18 g) favorite sweet dry rub
½ cup (120 ml) barbecue sauce

YOU COULD SKIP THE BRINING PROCESS here and still end up with a tasty meal. But trust me: The rich, homey flavor of the carrot, onion, and garlic in the brine really does make these chicken breasts taste perfect—especially when you layer on the rustic flavor of wood smoke.

1 In a large bowl, combine the water, salt, sugar, carrot, onion, garlic, bay leaves, and peppercorns and stir until the salt dissolves. Add the chicken breasts, cover, and brine in the refrigerator for 4 hours.

2 Take the chicken breasts out of the brine and pat them dry using paper towels.

3 Preheat the smoker to 250°F (120°C), using hardwood smoking chips (cherry, hickory, oak, or applewood).

4 Heat the oil in a large skillet over medium-high heat and brown the chicken breasts on all sides, turning once, about 5 minutes total.

5 Season the chicken with the dry rub and place them in the smoker skin-side up. Smoke until the internal temperature reaches 150°F (66°C), about 1 hour. Brush the breasts with barbecue sauce and continue to smoke until the internal temperature reaches 165°F (74°C), about 30 minutes longer.

6 Let the chicken breasts rest for 10 minutes before serving.

Smoked CHICKEN THIGHS

SERVES 4

PREP TIME: 15 minutes
COOK TIME: 1 ½ hours

2 tablespoons (25 g) brown sugar
1 teaspoon smoked paprika
1 teaspoon salt
½ teaspoon freshly ground black pepper
½ teaspoon garlic powder
½ teaspoon onion powder
½ teaspoon dry mustard powder
⅛ teaspoon cayenne pepper
8 bone-in, skin-on chicken thighs
½ cup (120 ml) apple cider vinegar
¼ cup (60 ml) water
2 tablespoons (30 ml) barbecue sauce

I SOMETIMES THINK OF CHICKEN THIGHS as chicken breasts on a budget. If your crew wants white-meat chicken but inflation is making breasts a little too pricey, get in the thigh habit. And why not start with this simple and easy smoke-cooked version?

1 Preheat the smoker to 275°F (140°C), using hardwood smoking chips (hickory, oak, or applewood).

2 In a small bowl, mix together the brown sugar, paprika, salt, pepper, garlic powder, onion powder, mustard powder, and cayenne. Pat the chicken dry with paper towels and rub them with the spice mixture.

3 In a small bowl, whisk together the vinegar, water, and barbecue sauce until blended and set aside.

4 Arrange the thighs skin-side up in the smoker and smoke for 45 minutes. Baste the thighs with the vinegar mixture and continue smoking, basting every 15 minutes, until the internal temperature is 165°F (74°C), about 45 minutes longer.

5 Let the thighs rest for 10 minutes before serving.

Smoked
CHICKEN DRUMSTICKS

SERVES 4

PREP TIME: 15 minutes, plus marinating time
COOK TIME: 1 ½ hours

3 tablespoons (38 g) packed brown sugar

1 tablespoon (17 g) salt

2 teaspoons smoked paprika

2 teaspoons ground cumin

2 teaspoons garlic powder

1 teaspoon freshly ground black pepper

¼ teaspoon cayenne pepper

8 chicken drumsticks

1 tablespoon (15 ml) olive oil

WHENEVER I HAVE A GROUP TO FEED that includes kids, I make these drumsticks. Kids seem to like the idea of a food they can hold in their hands and does not require a fork and knife. Jack up the amounts of cumin and cayenne for a spicier version—or reduce them, if you like, if you think the young'uns can't handle the heat.

1 In a small bowl, mix together the brown sugar, salt, paprika, cumin, garlic powder, pepper, and cayenne. Pat the chicken dry with paper towels and rub them with the oil. Sprinkle the seasoning all over them and place the drumsticks on a plate. Refrigerate the chicken, uncovered, for at least 2 hours or up to overnight.

2 Preheat the smoker to 275°F (140°C), using hardwood smoking chips (hickory, oak, or applewood).

3 Remove the drumsticks from the refrigerator and bring them to room temperature.

4 Arrange the drumsticks in the smoker and smoke until the internal temperature is 165°F (74°C), about 1½ hours.

5 Let the drumsticks rest for 10 minutes before serving.

CHICKEN WINGS
from the Smoker

SERVES 2

PREP TIME: *10 minutes*
COOK TIME: *2 hours*

2 tablespoons (12 g)
    smoked paprika
1 ½ tablespoons (9 g)
    freshly ground black
    pepper
1 ½ tablespoons (6 g)
    garlic powder
1 tablespoon (17 g) salt
2 ½ pounds (1,140 g)
    chicken wings

IF THE CRAVING FOR SMOKED CHICKEN WINGS hits you, these wings bring together the delectable essence of a smokehouse while adding an additional layer of irresistibly crunchy skin!

1 In a large bowl, stir together the paprika, pepper, garlic powder, and salt. Add the chicken wings and toss to coat in the seasonings. Let them sit for 15 minutes at room temperature.

2 Preheat the smoker to 250°F (120°C), using hardwood smoking chips (hickory, oak, or applewood).

3 Arrange the wings in the smoker, leaving space between them, and smoke until the internal temperature is 165°F (74°C), about 2 hours.

4 Remove from smoker and let the wings rest for 10 minutes before serving.

Classic
BEER CAN CHICKEN

SERVES 4

PREP TIME: 15 minutes
COOK TIME: 5 to 6 hours

2 tablespoons (25 g) brown sugar
2 teaspoons chipotle chili powder
2 teaspoons paprika
1 teaspoon garlic powder
½ teaspoon onion powder
½ teaspoon salt
¼ teaspoon freshly ground black
   pepper
One 4 ½-pound (2 kg) whole
   chicken, giblets removed
Olive oil
One 12-ounce (360 ml) can beer,
   half full

THIS IS A CLASSIC RECIPE, at least as of about twenty years ago when it really took off in popularity, and an exciting one for everyone to watch cook! The beer imparts a distinct flavor and makes the chicken juicy-moist, perfect for a hot summer evening outdoors.

1 Preheat the smoker to 225°F (107°C), using hardwood smoking chips (hickory, oak, or applewood).

2 In a small bowl, mix together the brown sugar, chili powder, paprika, garlic powder, onion powder, salt, and pepper.

3 Pat the chicken dry with paper towels and rub with olive oil. Season the chicken with the spice mixture.

4 Place the beer can on a baking sheet and position the chicken with the can in the cavity so it sits upright. Put the chicken in the smoker and smoke until the internal temperature is 165°F (74°C), 5 to 6 hours. For a crispy skin, increase the smoker temperature to 350°F (180°C) in the last hour of cooking.

5 Let the chicken rest for 15 minutes before serving.

Bourbon BBQ
SMOKED CHICKEN WINGS

SERVES 4

PREP TIME: *20 minutes*
COOK TIME: *2 hours and 25 minutes*

2 tablespoons (30 ml) olive oil
½ small sweet onion, finely
    chopped
1 tablespoon (8 g) minced garlic
1 ½ cups (360 ml) ketchup
½ cup (120 ml) bourbon
One 6-ounce (168 g) can tomato
    paste
⅓ cup (65 g) packed brown sugar
¼ cup (60 ml) apple cider vinegar
2 tablespoons (30 ml)
    Worcestershire sauce
2 tablespoons (30 ml) liquid smoke
1 teaspoon salt
½ teaspoon freshly ground black
    pepper
4 pounds (1.8 kg) chicken wings,
    patted dry
2 tablespoons (30 ml) olive oil
3 tablespoons (18 g) chicken dry
    rub (your favorite)

THERE IS SOMETHING MAGICAL, for me at least, in the way the crisp skin on smoked wings absorbs the flavor of the bourbon, as if it was always meant to be there.

1 In a medium saucepan, heat the olive oil over medium-high heat. Add the onion and sauté until softened, about 3 minutes. Add the garlic and sauté for 2 minutes. Whisk in the ketchup, bourbon, tomato paste, brown sugar, vinegar, Worcestershire sauce, liquid smoke, salt, and pepper and bring to a boil. Reduce the heat to low, partially cover, and simmer until thickened, about 15 minutes. Allow the sauce to cool and set aside.

2 Preheat the smoker to 250°F (120°C), using hardwood smoking chips (hickory, oak, or applewood).

3 Pat the chicken wings dry with a paper towel and place them in a large bowl. Add the olive oil and toss to coat. Add the dry rub and massage it in with your hands.

4 Arrange the wings in the smoker, leaving space between them, and smoke until the internal temperature is 165°F (74°C), about 2 hours.

5 Baste the wings with the sauce and smoke for 5 minutes, flip them, baste again, and smoke for 5 minutes.

6 Allow the wings to rest for 10 minutes and serve with the remaining barbecue sauce.

Brined
SMOKED TURKEY

SERVES 8

PREP TIME: *30 minutes, plus 24 hours brining time*
COOK TIME: *About 8 hours*

1 gallon (3.8 L) hot water
4 cups (960 ml) apple cider vinegar
½ cup salt, plus more if needed
2 tablespoons (12 g) black peppercorns
2 tablespoons (8 g) chopped fresh thyme
1 tablespoon (4 g) chopped fresh sage
2 bay leaves
One 15-pound (6.8 kg) turkey, neck and giblets removed
¾ cup (168 g) unsalted butter, at room temperature
2 teaspoons dried thyme
2 teaspoons dried rosemary
1 teaspoon dried sage
1 teaspoon freshly ground black pepper, plus more as needed
½ teaspoon garlic powder
2 tablespoons (30 ml) olive oil

IF YOU'RE FORTUNATE ENOUGH TO LIVE in a place that's not buried in snow by November, consider taking your holiday turkey outside for this amazing version. You're gonna love it! You might never cook another turkey in your oven again.

1   In a large food-safe bucket that will fit in your refrigerator, combine the water, apple cider vinegar, salt, peppercorns, fresh thyme, fresh sage, and bay leaves and stir until the salt dissolves. Add the turkey, cover, and brine in the refrigerator overnight.

2   Preheat the smoker to 250°F (120°C), using hardwood smoking chips (cherry, hickory, oak, or applewood).

3   In a small bowl, mix together the butter, dried thyme, dried rosemary, dried sage, pepper, and garlic powder until blended.

4   Remove the turkey from the brine, rinse it in cold water, and pat it dry with paper towels. Place the turkey breast-side up in a large foil roasting pan. Lift the turkey skin gently and rub the butter mixture all over under the skin. Rub the outside skin with olive oil and season with salt and pepper.

5   Place the turkey in the smoker and smoke for about 30 minutes per pound (455 g), or until the internal temperature is 165°F (74°C) in the thickest part of the breast meat, about 8 hours for a 15-pound (6.8 kg) bird.

6   Remove the turkey from the smoker, tent it with foil, and let it rest for 30 minutes before serving.

CHAPTER

Two

HERE'S THE BEEF

FROM THE

Grill

Your Best BURGERS

SERVES 4

PREP TIME: *15 minutes*
COOK TIME: *16 minutes*

1 pound (455 g) ground beef (80/20)
Salt and freshly ground black pepper
Sliced cheese
4 hamburger buns, toasted
Sliced tomato
Sliced onion (red or white)
Sliced pickles
Lettuce leaves
Condiments

I BELIEVE IN FREEDOM AT THE GRILL. That's why I do not micro-manage all your choices in this recipe, instead giving you a lot of room to personalize the burgers to your taste. That's why I call them *Your* Best Burgers. Swiss cheese or Cheddar or blue? You decide. A kaiser bun, a sesame bun, a whole wheat bun, or a traditional white bun? Red onion versus yellow versus sweet? You know better than I what you and the people you cook for like. I like them all, and you get to choose.

1 Preheat the grill to medium-high heat, around 400°F (200°C). Clean the grill grates thoroughly.

2 Separate the beef into four equal pieces and shape them into ¾-inch (2 cm) thick patties. Season all sides of the patties with salt and pepper.

3 Grill the burgers for 3 minutes to sear them, flip, and sear the other side for 3 minutes. Then continue cooking the burgers until they are the desired doneness, turning once halfway through, about 10 minutes longer for medium-well.

4 If you are making cheeseburgers, add the cheese slices during the last minute of cooking to melt them.

5 Serve the burgers on toasted buns with your favorite toppings and condiments.

Perfectly GRILLED STEAK

SERVES 4

PREP TIME: 5 minutes
COOK TIME: 10 to 12 minutes

Four 12-ounce (340 g) New
    York strip or boneless rib-
    eye steaks, about 1 ½ inches
    (3.8 cm) thick, trimmed
Olive oil
Salt and freshly ground
    black pepper

COUNT ME AMONG THE STEAK LOVERS who think the best steaks are not all fancied up with sauces and rubs but simple preparations that let the meat speak for itself. Salt, fresh-cracked pepper, and a little olive oil do the trick here.

1 Let the steaks sit out at room temperature for 30 minutes before grilling.

2 Preheat the grill to high heat, about 450°F (230°C).

3 Brush the steaks with oil and season them generously with salt and pepper.

4 Grill the steaks until nicely seared, 4 to 5 minutes. Flip them over and grill for 3 to 5 minutes for medium-rare (135°F [57°C] internal temperature) or 5 to 7 minutes for medium (140°F [60°C] internal temperature).

5 Transfer the steaks to a cutting board and let rest for 10 minutes before serving.

Stuffed
BURGERS WITH A WHISKEY & CHEESE FILLING

SERVES 4

PREP TIME: 25 minutes, plus
overnight chilling
COOK TIME: 20 minutes

For the Patties
½ pound (227 g) ground beef
½ pound (227 g) ground pork
¼ cup (40 g) finely chopped onion
2 tablespoons (10 g) bread crumbs
1 tablespoon (15 ml)
    Worcestershire sauce
1 teaspoon minced garlic
Salt and freshly ground black pepper

For the Whiskey & Cheese Filling
1 cup (120 g) shredded sharp
    Cheddar cheese
1 tablespoon (15 ml) whiskey
1 shallot, minced
1 teaspoon minced garlic

For the Burgers
4 hamburger buns with sesame
    seeds, toasted
Sliced tomato
Sliced onion (red or white)
Sliced pickles
Lettuce leaves
Condiments

WHISKEY AND BEEF ARE A CHAMPION PAIR. The half-pork, half-beef meat combo also is a winner in my book—and once you try it, it might well become your go-to burger base. I've seen it happen!

1 To make the patties, the day before, in a large bowl, mix the beef, pork, onion, bread crumbs, Worcestershire sauce, and garlic until very well combined. Form the mixture into eight ½-inch (1.3 cm) thick patties and set aside.

2 To make the filling, in a medium bowl, mix together the shredded cheese, whiskey, shallot, and garlic until well combined and almost a paste. Place 1 tablespoon (15 g) of the filling on four of the patties, placing it right in the middle of each. Top them with the remaining four patties and pinch the sides to seal the filling inside the meat. Cover the patties or put them in an airtight container and refrigerate overnight. Refrigerate the remaining filling.

3 Preheat the grill to medium-high heat, around 400°F (200°C). Clean the grill grates thoroughly and place a drip pan under one side.

4 Season all sides of the patties with salt and pepper and grill the burgers for 10 minutes (with the lid down), flip them, and grill the other side for 5 minutes. Top the burgers with the remaining filling and grill until cooked through, about 5 minutes longer.

5 To assemble the burgers, serve on toasted buns with your favorite toppings and condiments.

GRILLED TRI-TIP,
Straight Up

SERVES 6

PREP TIME: 5 minutes
COOK TIME: 1 hour and 12 minutes

One 3-pound (1,365 g) tri-tip roast
Level Up B Rub or other barbecue
    rub for beef

IT VARIES FROM PLACE TO PLACE and depends on market conditions, but in general if you're looking for steak-like flavor at much lower prices, a hunk of tri-tip is where you should go. Serve with Grilled Asparagus (page 148) and some simple rice or grilled corn on the cob and a tangy slaw and you've got yourself an easy and pretty darn fancy dinner without a lot of effort.

1 Preheat the grill to medium heat, about 350°F (180°C), using half the burners on one side (leaving the other burners off).

2 Season the roast generously on all sides with the rub. Place the roast on the grill's cool side, close the grill lid, and cook for about 1 hour, turning the meat every 10 minutes, for medium-rare.

3 When the meat reaches an internal temperature of 120°F (49°C), move it to the hot side and grill for 3 minutes per side to create a nicely browned surface.

4 Remove the meat to a cutting board, let it rest for 10 minutes, slice the beef thinly against the grain, and serve.

Grilled
TRI-TIP IN A CLASSIC BBQ MARINADE

SERVES 6

PREP TIME: 10 minutes, plus marinating time
COOK TIME: 40 minutes

¼ cup (60 ml) olive oil
1 tablespoon (2 g) dried parsley
1 tablespoon (15 g) seasoning salt
2 teaspoons garlic powder
2 teaspoons brown sugar
1 teaspoon onion powder
1 teaspoon freshly ground black
    pepper
One 2 ½-pound (1,138 g) tri-tip
    roast

THIS IS A MARINADE I OFTEN USE when I am making traditional barbecue in a smoker. Guess what! It works its same magic on grilled things, too, like this flame-kissed tri-tip.

1 In a large resealable plastic bag, mix the olive oil, parsley, seasoning salt, garlic powder, brown sugar, onion powder, and pepper. Add the roast to the bag, press out as much air as possible, seal, and massage the mixture all over the meat. Refrigerate for at least 2 hours and up to 8 hours.

2 Let the meat rest in the bag at room temperature for 30 minutes before grilling.

3 Preheat the grill to high heat, about 450°F (230°C). Turn half the burners off, creating a cooler (indirect heat) side.

4 Remove the roast from the bag and discard the marinade. Sear the roast on the hot side of the grill for 2 to 3 minutes on each side. Transfer the meat to the indirect heat side and drop the temperature to low, about 300°F (150°C). Shut the grill lid and cook for about 30 minutes for medium-rare, until the internal temperature reaches 145°F (63°C).

5 Remove the roast from the grill, tent loosely with foil, let rest for 10 minutes, slice against the grain, and serve.

Smoked
BEEF CHUCK FROM THE GRILL

SERVES 4 TO 6

PREP TIME: *15 minutes*
COOK TIME: *9 ½ to 10 hours*

¼ cup (50 g) coarsely ground black pepper
¼ cup (68 g) salt
One 4- to 5-pound (1.8 to 2.3 kg) beef chuck roll

MY FRIENDS WHO DO NOT YET OWN a smoker often ask me if they should get one. I always say yes—but I also tell them they can rig up a standard backyard grill to do some smoking, by what is known as the indirect heat or indirect cooking method. This simple presentation of inexpensive beef chuck shows how you can add real smoke flavor with this method. If you do have a smoker, just follow the time and temperature directions for your smoker.

1 In a small bowl, mix the pepper and salt. Rub the pepper mixture all over the beef until it's evenly coated.

2 Tie the chuck roll with twine, wrapping it up at 1-inch (2.5 cm) intervals, and set aside to fire up the smoker.

3 Preheat the grill to medium-high heat, about 400°F (200°C), using half the burners on one side (leaving the other burners off). Don't forget to give the grill grate a good cleaning and a rub with a little oil!

4 Place the beef on the grill's cool side. Wrap 2 or 3 hardwood chunks in aluminum foil and place them on the hot side of the grill.

5 Cover the grill and let the beef soak in that smoky goodness for about 4 hours. Keep the grill temperature between 275° and 300°F (140° and 150°C) by adjusting the knobs. Add more wood as needed to maintain the smoke.

6 Once the beef has a dark bark on the outside and the internal temperature is 150° to 165°F (66° to 74°C), remove the meat from the grill and wrap it tightly in heavy-duty aluminum foil.

7 Place the wrapped beef back on the cooler side of the grill and cook for 5 to 5 ½ hours between 225° and 250°F (107° and 120°C).

8 Remove the foil and place the meat back on the cooler grill side until a crispy bark forms, about 30 minutes.

CONTINUED ➡

9 Transfer the beef to a cutting board, cover with foil, and let it cool for about 30 minutes before carving it.

10 Following the grain, cut the meat in half, take off the twine, and place the halves cut-side down on the cutting board. Slice the beef thinly against the grain and serve.

PRO TIP: Slice only what you plan to eat, wrap up the leftovers in foil, and refrigerate the meat for up to 1 week.

AB's Classic
CHILI DOGS

SERVES 6

PREP TIME: *5 minutes*
COOK TIME: *30 minutes*

For the Chili
1 ½ pounds (680 g) ground beef
3 to 4 cups (720 to 960 ml) water
½ medium yellow onion, finely
    chopped or minced
2 tablespoons (30 ml) ketchup
1 teaspoon bottled hot sauce
½ teaspoon Worcestershire sauce
2 tablespoons (12 g) chili powder
1 teaspoon salt
½ teaspoon freshly ground
    black pepper
1 teaspoon onion powder
½ teaspoon paprika
¼ teaspoon sugar
¼ cup (60 ml) beer (optional)
2 tablespoons (30 g) tomato paste

For the Hot Dogs
6 good-quality hot dogs
6 hot dog buns
Mayonnaise (optional)

EVERYONE, YOUNG AND OLD, seems to enjoy my signature recipe for chili dogs, and I know you will too.

1   To make the chili, place the ground beef in a large pot and cover with the water. Break up the meat into small pieces with a spatula. Place over medium-high heat on the stovetop. Add the diced onion, ketchup, hot sauce, Worcestershire sauce, chili powder, salt, pepper, onion powder, paprika, sugar, and beer (if using) and bring to a boil. Reduce the heat and simmer, uncovered, until the chili is no longer watery, about 15 minutes. Stir the chili occasionally. Stir in the tomato paste to thicken and set the chili aside.

2   To make the hot dogs, preheat the grill to medium heat, about 350°F (180°C). Lightly oil the grill grates.

3   Grill the hot dogs, turning them a few times, until they are partially but not completely charred, about 5 minutes.

4   Toast the buns on the grill for about 30 seconds. Add mayonnaise if you like and serve the hot dogs on the buns and with the chili on top. Serve hot.

Big-Flavor STEAK KABOBS

SERVES 4

PREP TIME: *25 minutes, plus marinating time*
COOK TIME: *10 minutes*

For the Marinade
¼ cup (60 ml) olive oil
2 tablespoons (30 ml) balsamic vinegar
2 tablespoons (30 ml) Worcestershire sauce
1 tablespoon (15 ml) fresh lime juice
1 tablespoon (15 ml) maple syrup
2 teaspoons minced garlic
1 teaspoon onion powder
1 teaspoon dried oregano
¼ teaspoon salt
⅛ teaspoon freshly ground black pepper

For the Kabobs
1 ½ pounds (680 g) sirloin steak, cut into 1-inch (2.5 cm) cubes
2 bell peppers (any color), seeded and cut into 1-inch (2.5 cm) chunks
1 red onion, cut into 1-inch (2.5 cm) pieces
8 medium button mushrooms
8 metal skewers or long wooden skewers soaked in water overnight

SWEETNESS FROM THE BALSAMIC and the maple syrup, some bite from the lime and garlic, and some earthy umami from the oregano, onion powder, and Worcestershire sauce really make these kabobs sing.

1 To make the marinade, in a medium bowl, whisk together the oil, vinegar, Worcestershire sauce, lime juice, maple syrup, garlic, onion powder, oregano, salt, and pepper.

2 To make the kabobs, add the steak to the bowl or marinade, toss to coat, cover, and refrigerate for at least 1 hour and up to 8 hours.

3 Preheat the grill to high heat, about 450°F (230°C).

4 Thread the marinated meat with the bell peppers, onion, and mushrooms onto skewers, alternating the pieces and keeping a small space between the ingredients so they can cook evenly. Brush the kabobs with the remaining marinade and discard what is left.

5 Grill the kabobs for 8 to 10 minutes, until the meat reaches your desired doneness, turning them to get all the sides. Let the kabobs rest for 10 minutes before serving.

New World
CARNE ASADA TACOS

SERVES 4

PREP TIME: *20 minutes, plus marinating time*
COOK TIME: *10 minutes*

For the Marinade
⅓ cup (80 ml) olive oil
Juice of 1 large orange
Juice of 4 limes
¼ cup (8 g) chopped cilantro
2 tablespoons (25 g) brown sugar
2 tablespoons (30 ml) soy sauce
1 tablespoon (8 g) minced garlic
1 ½ teaspoons dried oregano
1 ½ teaspoons chili powder
1 teaspoon ground cumin
½ teaspoon salt
½ teaspoon freshly ground black
  pepper

For the Tacos
1 pound (455 g) skirt steak
8 small flour tortillas
Chopped onion
Guacamole
Sliced radish
Chopped cilantro
Cotija cheese

EVERYONE KNOWS THAT *CARNE* **MEANS** "meat." But do you know what *asada* means? That turns out to be a little complicated. In Spanish the term can mean either "roasted" or "grilled"—two different cooking techniques. What makes it even more complicated is that in Mexican restaurants nowadays, *asada* usually refers to meat, almost always beef, that is marinated in a mixture of spices and aromatics like the ones you see in this recipe and then cooked in any manner, from roasting or broiling to braising or grilling. In recent years this last meaning has come to be the most popular one, and the older meanings of simply roasted or grilled are falling out of favor.

1 To make the marinade, combine the olive oil, orange juice, lime juice, cilantro, brown sugar, soy sauce, garlic, oregano, chili powder, cumin, salt, and pepper in a large resealable plastic bag.

2 To make the tacos, add the steak to the bag of marinade, press out as much air as possible, seal, and refrigerate for at least 8 hours and up to 24 hours.

3 Preheat the grill to high, about 450°F (230°C). Clean and oil the grates.

4 Remove the steak from the bag and discard the marinade. Grill the steak with the lid closed for 2 minutes, flip, close the lid, and grill for another 2 minutes to sear both sides. Reduce the heat to medium, about 350°F (180°C), and grill until it reaches your desired doneness, about 6 more minutes, turning halfway through, for medium-rare (135°F [57°C] internal temperature).

5 Transfer the steak to a cutting board and let it rest for 10 minutes before cutting against the grain into thin slices.

6 Serve the meat in warmed tortillas with your favorite toppings.

Borderland
STEAK FAJITAS

SERVES 4

PREP TIME: *15 minutes, plus marinating time*
COOK TIME: *12 minutes*

2 pounds (910 g) flank steak
Juice of 2 large limes
6 tablespoons (90 ml) olive oil
3 large cloves garlic, grated
1 tablespoon (6 g) chili powder
2 teaspoons ground cumin
½ teaspoon paprika
½ teaspoon garlic powder
½ teaspoon onion powder
¼ teaspoon cayenne pepper (optional)
2 teaspoons salt
2 large bell peppers (any color), seeded and sliced
1 medium onion, sliced
Freshly ground black pepper
8 small flour tortillas
Toppings, as desired

DEPENDING ON WHERE YOU LIVE, flank steak might not be called that but instead be called London broil or skirt steak. Whatever its name, it is the ideal meat for fajitas, because of its natural juiciness and because it cuts well into thin slices, which not all steaks do. For the thinnest and best slices, cut against the grain, which means your knife is perpendicular to the natural lines you see on the surface of the meat.

1 Add the flank steak to a large resealable plastic bag. Add the lime juice, 4 tablespoons (60 ml) of the olive oil, grated garlic, chili powder, cumin, paprika, garlic powder, onion powder, and cayenne (if using) to the bag. Seal the bag, pressing out the air, and massage the marinade into the meat. Refrigerate the meat for at least 2 hours and up to 8 hours.

2 Preheat the grill to high heat, about 450°F (230°C). Place a grill pan or baking sheet on one side of the grill.

3 Remove the steak from the bag, discarding the marinade, and sprinkle the meat with 1 ½ teaspoons of the salt on both sides.

4 Add the peppers and onion to a medium bowl and toss with the remaining 2 tablespoons (30 ml) of olive oil, remaining ½ teaspoon of salt, and a couple pinches of black pepper.

5 Add the pepper mixture to the grill pan. Cook for 3 to 4 minutes and then add the steak to the uncovered side of the grill. Use tongs to toss the veggies and close the grill.

6 Grill the steak for about 4 minutes and flip it over. Toss the pepper mixture again, and if it is charred to your preference, remove it from the grill to a plate and set it aside.

7 Cook the steak for another 3 to 4 minutes or until it reaches your desired doneness. For flank steak, medium-rare to medium (internal temperature of 140 to 145°F [60° to 63°C]) is perfect. The temperature will increase 5°F (3°C) as it rests.

CONTINUED ➡

8 Remove the steak and pepper mixture (if you haven't already done this) from the grill. Let the steak rest for 10 minutes before using a sharp knife to cut the meat against the grain into thin slices.

9 Serve the steak and veggies in warm tortillas with your favorite toppings.

Grilled
MEATBALL SOUP

SERVES 6 AS A FIRST COURSE, 4 TO 6 AS A MAIN COURSE

PREP TIME: *25 minutes*
COOK TIME: *40 minutes*

For the Meatballs
1 pound (455 g) lean ground beef
1 tablespoon (2 g) dried parsley
2 teaspoons garlic powder
2 teaspoons granulated onion
1 teaspoon salt
½ teaspoon freshly ground black
   pepper
Pinch of cayenne pepper

For the Soup
1 tablespoon (15 ml) olive oil
1 sweet onion, diced
3 celery stalks, finely chopped
2 carrots, diced
2 teaspoons minced garlic
6 cups (1,440 ml) beef broth
2 cups (480 ml) tomato sauce
1 large russet potato, diced
4 cups (120 g) chopped spinach
Sea salt and freshly ground
   black pepper

IF YOU ARE PINCHED FOR TIME most weekdays, grill up a batch of these meatballs on the weekend, store them in the refrigerator, and then make the rest of the soup at the end of a busy workday. Better yet, grill up a double batch and store half in the freezer either for another use or to make this soup a second time.

1 Preheat the grill to medium-low heat, about 300°F (150°C). Turn half the burners off.

2 To make the meatballs, in a medium bowl, mix together the beef, parsley, garlic powder, granulated onion, salt, pepper, and cayenne. Shape into 1-inch (2.5 cm) balls and arrange them on a grill pan or grill basket.

3 Place the grill pan on the cool side of the grill and close the lid. Cook until the meatballs are browned and cooked through, turning them to get all the sides, about 15 minutes. Remove the meatballs from the grill and set aside.

4 To make the soup, in a large stockpot over medium-high heat, heat the olive oil. Add the onion, celery, and carrots and sauté until softened, about 6 minutes. Add the garlic and sauté for 2 minutes longer.

5 Stir in the beef broth and tomato sauce and bring the soup to a boil. Add the potatoes and meatballs and simmer until the potatoes are tender and the soup thickens, about 15 minutes.

6 Remove the soup from the heat and stir in the spinach until it wilts, about 2 minutes.

7 Season with salt and pepper and serve.

Camp-Style
FOIL-PACK STEAK & POTATOES

SERVES 4

PREP TIME: *15 minutes*
COOK TIME: *25 minutes*

Salt
1 pound (455 g) baby potatoes, cut
    into ½-inch (1.3 cm) pieces
1 ½ pounds (680 g) sirloin steak
Level Up B Rub or your favorite
    steak seasoning
1 medium onion, halved and thinly
    sliced
2 tablespoons (8 g) chopped fresh
    parsley
1 tablespoon (15 ml) olive oil
1 tablespoon (8 g) minced garlic
1 tablespoon (4 g) Italian seasoning
Freshly ground black pepper
2 tablespoons (28 g) cold unsalted
    butter, cubed

CAMPERS AND RVERS LOVE FOIL-PACK COOKING. It's a popular way to grill in the great outdoors. Personally, I think all grillers should do more foil-pack grilling, even if they are in their own backyard: The enclosed packet forces the various flavors to marry and complement each other in an intensely flavorful way.

1 Preheat the grill to high heat, about 450°F (230°C).

2 Fill a large saucepan three-quarters full of water and add a pinch of salt. Bring the water to a boil over high heat and add the potatoes. Cook the potatoes for 5 minutes, drain, and transfer to a large bowl. Let them sit until they are cool enough to handle, about 10 minutes.

3 Cut the steak into pieces, 2 ½ to 3 inches (6 to 7.5 cm) for well done, 3 to 4 inches (7.5 to 10 cm) for medium, 5 inches (12.5 cm) for rare. Season the chunks with Level Up B Rub.

4 Add the steak, onion, parsley, olive oil, garlic, Italian seasoning, salt, and pepper to the bowl with the potatoes and toss well.

5 Set out four pieces of aluminum foil, each at least 12 inches (30.5 cm) square. Evenly divide the steak and potato mixture among the foil sheets. Top each with butter cubes, then fold the foil over the steak and potatoes to form a packet and seal well.

6 Place the packets on the grill and cook for 8 to 10 minutes per side, or until the potatoes are tender. The exact grilling time can vary depending on the type of foil used, the grill temperature, and the size of the steak chunks. Open the packets carefully and enjoy.

Grill-Roasted
BBQ POT ROAST

SERVES 6

PREP TIME: 10 minutes
COOK TIME: 2 hours and 40 minutes

One 3-pound (1365 g) pot roast
Salt and freshly ground black
    pepper
2 tablespoons (30 ml) olive oil
1 onion, cut into 1-inch (2.5 cm)
    slices
2 cups (480 ml) barbecue sauce
    (your favorite)

AS FAR AS I KNOW, NO ONE'S EVER won a barbecue competition with pot roast as their entry. But the cut takes well to the grill and is an inexpensive way to feed a crowd.

1   Preheat the grill to medium heat, about 350°F (180°C).

2   If the roast is already tied with butcher's twine leave in place. If not, use butcher's twine to tie the roast into a more compact package. Season the roast generously with salt and pepper.

3   Heat the olive oil in a Dutch oven over medium-high heat and sear the roast on all sides, about 2 minutes per side.

4   Remove the Dutch oven from the heat and arrange the onion slices in the bottom, then place the roast on the onion. Pour the barbecue sauce over the beef.

5   Cover the Dutch oven and place it on the grill, close the grill lid, and cook until the meat is fork-tender, about 2 ½ hours, turning the meat halfway through. Serve.

GRILLED STEAK SANDWICHES
with Horseradish Sauce

SERVES 4

PREP TIME: 10 minutes
COOK TIME: 9 minutes

Four 5-ounce (140 g) sirloin steaks
Olive oil
Salt and freshly ground black pepper
4 kaiser rolls, halved
¼ cup (60 ml) sour cream
1 tablespoon (15 g) prepared
    horseradish
1 teaspoon Dijon mustard
1 teaspoon apple cider vinegar
1 tablespoon (2 g) chopped
    fresh chives

SIRLOIN STEAKS HAVE MUCH OF the high-end flavor of a T-bone or rib-eye steak without the high-end price. They also slice easily when cooked. For those reasons, they're my go-to choice for grilled steak sandwiches.

1 Preheat the grill to medium-high heat, about 400°F (200°C).

2 Lightly brush the steaks with olive oil and season them with salt and pepper. Grill the steaks until they reach the desired doneness, turning once, about 4 minutes per side for medium-rare.

3 Remove the steaks from the grill and let them rest for 10 minutes.

4 Turn the grill off and place the buns, cut-side down, on the grates. Heat until they are lightly toasted, about 1 minute, and remove them to your work surface.

5 While the steaks are resting, in a small bowl, mix together the sour cream, horseradish, mustard, vinegar, and chives until well combined. Season the sauce with salt and pepper. Slather the sauce on both sides of the buns.

6 Cut the steaks against the grain into thin slices and pile the meat on the buns. Serve.

FROM THE
Smoker

Slow-Smoked
MEATLOAF

SERVES 6

PREP TIME: 15 minutes
COOK TIME: 2 hours and 5 minutes

1 pound (455 g) ground beef
   (80/20 percent)
1 pound (455 g) ground pork
¾ cup (90 g) bread crumbs
2 large eggs
1 small red bell pepper, seeded and
   finely chopped
1 small onion, finely chopped
1 teaspoon minced garlic
2 tablespoons (16 g) AB's Burger
   Rub or AB's Level Up BBQ
   Seasoning, or your favorite
½ cup (120 ml) plus 2 tablespoons
   (30 ml) barbecue sauce

THE STANDARD MEATLOAF, COOKED IN A LOAF PAN in the oven, is timeless comfort food. I'll give you that. But from the first time I made a meatloaf infused with the deep flavors of wood smoke, I abandoned the oven and never looked back. If you think you left meatloaf behind a decade or two ago, give this easy recipe a try. You'll come back.

1 Preheat the smoker to 225°F (107°C), using hardwood smoking chips (hickory, oak, or applewood).

2 In a large bowl, mix together the beef, pork, bread crumbs, eggs, red pepper, onion, garlic, seasoning, and 2 tablespoons (30 ml) of the barbecue sauce. Form the meat mixture into a loaf shape, about 9 by 5 inches (23 by 12.5 cm), and place it on a piece of butcher paper.

3 Transfer the meatloaf and paper to the smoker, and smoke until the meatloaf reaches an internal temperature of 160°F (71°C), about 2 hours.

4 Brush the meatloaf with the remaining ½ cup (120 ml) of barbecue sauce and smoke for 5 minutes more. Serve.

Southern-Style
SMOKED & BRAISED OXTAILS

SERVES 4

PREP TIME: 15 minutes
COOK TIME: 4 ½ hours

5 pounds (2.3 kg) beef oxtails (6 to 8 pieces), trimmed of excess fat
¼ cup (25 g) Level Up BBQ Rub or your favorite
1 tablespoon (15 ml) olive oil
1 small onion, diced
1 carrot, diced
2 celery stalks, diced
1 tablespoon (8 g) minced garlic
3 cups (720 ml) beef broth
1 cup (240 ml) dry red wine
¼ cup (60 ml) balsamic vinegar
3 tablespoons (45 ml) Worcestershire sauce
2 tablespoons (30 g) tomato paste
1 teaspoon salt
1 teaspoon freshly ground black pepper
Cooked rice, for serving

FANCY BIG CITY RESTAURANTS "DISCOVERED" OXTAILS a decade or so ago. But anyone who knows Southern or African American barbecue traditions knows that oxtails have always been a popular delicacy, a cheap cut of meat that either wood smoke or an intense braising liquid could turn into something magical. Here we have *both*: smoking followed by braising.

1 Preheat the smoker to 275°F (140°C), using hardwood smoking chips (hickory, oak, or applewood).

2 Season the oxtails generously all over with the rub and place them in the smoker. Smoke them until they are a dark mahogany color, about 2 hours.

3 While the oxtails are smoking, heat the olive oil in a large saucepan over medium-high heat. Add the onion, carrot, and celery and sauté until softened, about 5 minutes. Add the garlic and sauté for 2 minutes longer.

4 Stir in the beef broth, wine, vinegar, Worcestershire sauce, tomato, salt, and pepper and bring to a boil. Decrease the heat to low and simmer for 10 minutes to reduce the braising liquid. Set it aside until the oxtails are ready.

5 Remove the oxtails from the smoker, arrange them in a large cast-iron skillet, pour in the braising liquid, and cover the skillet with foil. Place the skillet in the smoker and smoke until the oxtails are fork-tender, about 2 ½ hours.

6 Transfer the oxtails to a serving platter and strain the braising liquid. Serve the oxtails over rice with a generous ladle of the braising liquid.

Texas-Style
MUSTARD-RUBBED SMOKED BRISKET

SERVES 8

PREP TIME: 10 minutes
COOK TIME: 9 to 10 hours

½ cup (120 ml) grainy mustard
One 12-pound (5.5 kg) brisket, trimmed to ¼ inch (6 mm) of fat
Salt and freshly ground black pepper

LATELY EVERYONE'S AN EXPERT on Texas brisket, with all sorts of complicated ideas for rubs and sauces and mops and pastes. Some of those recipes are great, granted, but I think the best place to start—and, frankly, the best place to *end up*, even if you've smoked brisket a hundred times—is with a thick rub of your favorite spice-rich grainy mustard. That's all you really need.

1 Rub the mustard all over the meat and generously season it with salt and pepper. Let the brisket rest until it is at room temperature.

2 Preheat the smoker to 265°F (130°C), using hardwood smoking chips (oak, hickory, or applewood).

3 Place the brisket in the smoker, fat-side up, and smoke for about 5 hours to create a dark bark, with an internal temperature of 165°F (74°C).

4 Remove the meat from the smoker and wrap it in a double layer of butcher paper. Place the wrapped meat back in the smoker, fat-side up, insert a meat thermometer in the middle of the fat, and continue to smoke until it reads 200°F (93°C), about 4 hours.

5 Let the brisket rest for at least 1 hour still wrapped before opening the paper, slicing, and serving the meat.

BRISKET
Chili

SERVES 8

PREP TIME: 20 minutes
COOK TIME: 1 to 2 hours

1 tablespoon (15 ml) olive oil
1 onion, chopped
1 green bell pepper, seeded and
    diced
1 teaspoon minced garlic
2 pounds (910 g) smoked brisket
    (cut into small cubes)
One 28-ounce (784 g) can diced
    tomatoes, undrained
One 28-ounce (784 g) can tomato
    sauce
One 16-ounce (455 g) can red
    kidney beans, rinsed and drained
One 16-ounce (455 g) can navy
    beans, rinsed and drained
One 16-ounce (455 g) can black
    beans, rinsed and drained
2 tablespoons (12 g) chipotle chili
    powder
1 tablespoon (6 g) ground cumin
1 tablespoon (12 g) brown sugar
Salt and freshly ground black
    pepper

I NEVER SMOKE A BIG BRISKET WITHOUT making enough meat for leftovers. Sometimes the leftovers get repurposed into thick sandwiches. My favorite day two use is this chili. And yes, I am aware that many chili purists say "no beans" to beans in their chili. On this point, I am proudly a non-purist.

1   Preheat the grill to medium heat, about 350°F (180°C).

2   Place a large Dutch oven on the grill and add the olive oil. Add the onion and bell pepper and sauté until softened, about 5 minutes. Add the garlic and sauté for 2 minutes longer.

3   Add the brisket, tomatoes with juices, tomato sauce, kidney beans, navy beans, black beans, chili powder, cumin, and brown sugar, stirring gently to combine.

4   Reduce the grill heat to low, about 300°F (150°C), close the lid, and cook for 1 to 2 hours, stirring occasionally, until the chili is thickened and bubbly.

5   Season with salt and pepper and serve immediately with your favorite chili toppings.

Smoked
BEEF RIBS

SERVES 4

PREP TIME: 15 minutes
COOK TIME: 6 to 8 hours

3 to 4 pounds (1,365 to 1,820 g) beef ribs (well-marbled and bone-in)
1 cup (96 g) freshly ground black pepper
¼ cup (68 g) salt
2 tablespoons (14 g) garlic powder
2 tablespoons (14 g) onion powder
Level Up B Rub (optional)
¼ cup (60 ml) Worcestershire sauce

MY GRANDFATHER WAS A MASTER AT COOKING beef ribs and he was the one who first got me interested in cooking them. He showed me how to cook them low and slow in a classic pit barrel. Now, I'm a Texas-style fan, keeping it real with just salt and pepper. But he's got this collection of spices, and I follow suit, mimicking his moves, hoping to capture that essence. And it's all going down in his vintage pit barrel. Meat on one side, fiery coals on the flip. So, I dive headfirst into the Dino Ribs game, chasing that perfect beef rib. I realized its insanely simple—just fire-tending and patience are all it takes. Looking back, I'm realizing it was always more than cooking; it was a piece of our story.

1 Preheat the smoker to 275°F (140°C), using hardwood smoking chips (hickory, oak, or applewood).

2 Pat the beef ribs dry with paper towels and trim the excess fat from the top of the ribs—do not remove the membrane.

3 In a medium bowl, mix together the pepper, salt, garlic powder, onion powder, and Level Up B Rub (if using).

4 Coat the beef ribs with the Worcestershire sauce and then evenly rub in the spice mixture.

5 Place the seasoned beef ribs in the smoker, bone-side down, with space between them for smoke circulation. Close the lid and smoke the ribs for 6 to 8 hours, maintaining a consistent temperature of 275°F (140°C). Check the internal temperature of the ribs with a meat thermometer occasionally. The ribs are ready when they reach an internal temperature of 200° to 205°F (93° to 96°C) and the meat is tender enough to pull away from the bone.

6 Remove the smoked beef ribs from the smoker, tent with foil, and let rest for 15 minutes before slicing. Enjoy!

CHAPTER

Three

BODACIOUS PORK & LAMB

FROM THE
Grill

Dressed-Up SOUTHERN BLT

SERVES 1

PREP TIME: *10 minutes*
COOK TIME: *7 minutes*

4 strips bacon

2 slices thick-cut white bread

1 teaspoon unsalted butter

2 tablespoons (30 g) pimento cheese

1 small tomato, cut into ½-inch (1.3 cm) slices

Salt and freshly ground black pepper

1 Bibb, Boston, or iceberg lettuce leaf

SOUTHERNERS WILL ADD PIMENTO CHEESE to just about anything. But you don't have to be from the South to pick up that tasty habit. You'll be surprised how a couple of tablespoons of pimento cheese elevate this BLT into a better version of the classic sandwich.

1 Place a medium skillet over medium-high heat and cook the bacon until crispy, turning once, about 7 minutes. Transfer the bacon to paper towels to drain.

2 Grill or toast the bread to the desired brownness and spread with the butter and pimento cheese.

3 Layer the bacon and tomato slices evenly on one slice, seasoning with salt and pepper.

4 Top with the lettuce leaf and the remaining bread slice. Serve.

Grilled Honey-Mustard PORK CHOPS

SERVES 4

PREP TIME: *10 minutes, plus marinating time*
COOK TIME: *19 minutes*

¼ cup (60 ml) olive oil
3 tablespoons (45 ml) soy sauce
2 tablespoons (40 g) honey
1 tablespoon (8 g) minced garlic
1 tablespoon (15 ml) grainy
   mustard
Four 6-ounce (168 g) bone-in
   pork chops

I LIKE MY GRILLED STEAKS plain and simple, but I think grilled pork chops benefit from an extra boost of flavor. For extra mustard flavor—which is the way I like these—serve with some mustard at the table.

1 Add the olive oil, soy sauce, honey, garlic, and mustard to a large resealable plastic bag and shake to combine. Add the pork chops to the bag, squeeze out as much air as possible, seal, and massage the marinade into the meat. Refrigerate for at least 1 hour and up to 8 hours.

2 Preheat the grill to medium-high heat, about 400°F (200°C).

3 Sear the pork chops for 2 minutes per side and reduce the grill heat to medium, about 350°F (180°C).

4 Grill the pork until it is lightly charred and reaches an internal temperature of 145°F (63°C), turning several times, for about 15 minutes total time.

5 Remove the pork to a platter, tent it loosely with foil, and let it rest for 5 minutes before serving.

Hawaiian-Inspired
MARINATED PORK TENDERLOIN

SERVES 4

PREP TIME: *15 minutes, plus marinating time*
COOK TIME: *20 to 24 minutes*

½ cup (120 ml) pineapple juice
¼ cup (60 ml) olive oil
¼ cup (50 g) packed brown sugar
¼ cup (60 ml) ketchup
3 tablespoons (45 ml) soy sauce
3 tablespoons (45 ml) chili sauce
1 teaspoon garlic powder
1 teaspoon ground ginger
½ teaspoon paprika
¼ teaspoon salt
2 pounds (910 g) pork tenderloins, trimmed

MANY COOKS BEFORE ME HAVE NOTED the affinity between pineapple and pork tenderloin. But I like to add some savory sauces and spices to complement, and take the edge off, the sweetness of the pineapple. This is one of those fancy enough for company, easy enough for a busy weeknight recipes that you can't have too many of.

1 Place the pineapple juice, oil, brown sugar, ketchup, soy sauce, chili sauce, garlic powder, ginger, paprika, and salt in a large resealable plastic bag and shake to combine. Reserve ½ cup (120 ml) of the marinade.

2 Add the pork tenderloins, squeeze out as much air as possible, and seal the bag. Massage the marinade into the meat and refrigerate for at least 4 hours and up to overnight. Refrigerate the reserved sauce.

3 Take the pork out of the refrigerator at least 30 minutes before grilling.

4 Preheat the grill to medium-high heat, about 400°F (200°C). Clean and oil the grates.

5 Place the pork on the grill and discard the marinade. Grill, turning to cook all four sides of the meat, 5 to 6 minutes per side, until the meat reaches an internal temperature of 145°F (63°C), brushing with the reserved marinade. Serve.

Sweet & Sour
PORK SKEWERS

SERVES 6

PREP TIME: *30 minutes, plus marinating time*
COOK TIME: *15 minutes*

⅓ cup (80 ml) soy sauce

¼ cup (60 ml) apple cider vinegar

¼ cup (50 g) packed brown sugar

2 hot chiles, such as serranos (lower heat) or jalapeños (higher heat), seeded and thinly sliced

2 tablespoons (30 ml) Asian-style fish sauce

2 tablespoons (16 g) peeled and grated fresh ginger

½ teaspoon freshly ground black pepper

3 pounds (1365 g) boneless pork shoulder, cut into ¼-inch (6 mm) thick slices

2 cups (300 g) pineapple chunks

12 metal skewers or wooden skewers soaked in water for 30 minutes

MY OPINION: YOU CAN BUY A BOTTLE OF SOMETHING labeled "Sweet and Sour Sauce" and use it to marinate the pork. But what you'll get is mostly sweet, with a syrupy flavor that lacks the authentic Asian-restaurant flavor the marinade I use in this recipe has. The fresh ginger and chiles make a world of difference. Fish sauce is available in all Asian markets and, nowadays, in many supermarkets.

1 In a large bowl, combine the soy sauce, vinegar, brown sugar, chiles, fish sauce, ginger, and pepper. Add the pork slices to the bowl, toss to coat, and refrigerate for at least 3 hours and up to overnight.

2 Preheat the grill to medium-high heat, about 400°F (200°C), and lightly oil the grates.

3 Thread the pork slices onto half the skewers, leaving a bit of space to allow for even cooking. Discard the sauce in the bowl. Thread the pineapple chunks onto the remaining skewers.

4 Grill the pork skewers for a total of 15 minutes, turning often, until the meat is cooked through and lightly charred. Put the pineapple skewers on halfway through the time. Serve.

Grilled
ITALIAN SAUSAGE SANDWICH

SERVES 4

PREP TIME: 10 minutes
COOK TIME: 14 minutes

1 teaspoon olive oil
1 onion, halved and thinly sliced
1 bell pepper (red or yellow),
    seeded and julienned
One 8-ounce (225 g) package
    sliced cremini mushrooms
Four 4-ounce (112 g) Italian
    sausages
1 large baguette, cut into 4 equal
    pieces and halved lengthwise, or
    4 smaller sub rolls
4 teaspoons (20 ml) yellow
    mustard

AS YOU PROBABLY KNOW, most stores sell sweet and hot Italian sausages. Why don't I tell you which one to get for this recipe? Because I want you to decide. They are both perfect hot off the grill.

1 Preheat the grill to high heat, about 450°F (230°C).

2 Place a medium cast-iron skillet on one side of the grill and add the olive oil. Add the onion and sauté until softened, about 3 minutes. Add the bell pepper and sauté until lightly browned, about 4 minutes longer.

3 While the veggies are cooking, grill the sausages on the other half of the grill until they are cooked through, turning to get all sides, about 12 minutes total.

4 Remove the skillet and sausages from the grill—you can put them in the skillet with the veggies. Turn the grill off and lay the baguette pieces cut-side down on the grate until lightly toasted, about 1 minute.

5 Slather mustard on each bun, add a sausage, and top each with peppers and onions.

LEG OF LAMB
from the Grill

SERVES 12 TO 15

PREP TIME: 5 minutes, plus marinating time
COOK TIME: 1 hour

For the Marinade
¼ cup (60 ml) olive oil
¼ cup (60 ml) red wine
1 tablespoon (15 ml) balsamic vinegar
6 cloves garlic, minced
2 tablespoons (8 g) chopped fresh thyme
2 tablespoons (8 g) chopped fresh rosemary
2 teaspoons salt
2 teaspoons freshly ground black pepper

One 6- to 7-pound (2.7 to 3.2 kg) boneless leg of lamb, twine removed and butterflied

MOST OF THE LAMB AFICIONADOS I KNOW consider the leg the most flavorful cut—and the true test of a lamb cook's prowess. I won't argue with the first part. As for the second, it's really not that difficult. Just be sure to check the lamb for doneness (at least 145°F [63°C]), because the meat cooks unevenly due to the varying thickness of different parts of the leg.

1 To make the marinade, in a bowl, stir together the oil, red wine, vinegar, garlic, thyme, rosemary, salt, and pepper and transfer to a glass bowl or baking dish large enough to hold the leg of lamb.

2 Add the lamb to the marinade and use your fingers to rub the marinade over the entire surface of the meat. Cover with plastic wrap and marinate in the refrigerator for at least 4 hours or overnight.

3 Preheat the grill to 275°F (140°C). Create an indirect heat fire in your covered grill, massing the coals on one half of the grill, or, for gas, leaving the burners on one side off.

4 Transfer the leg of lamb to the cool side of the grill. Cook, covered, for 35 to 45 minutes, flipping the meat once after about 20 minutes, until the meat reaches an internal temperature of 145°F (63°C).

5 Move the meat to the hot side of the grill and sear it for 5 minutes on each side, so that it is slightly charred but not burnt. Remove the meat and let it rest for 10 to 15 minutes. Slice thin or thick, as you prefer, and serve hot.

Grill-Roasted
LAMB RIBS

SERVES 6 TO 8

PREP TIME: 10 minutes
COOK TIME: 1 hour and 25 minutes

2 to 2 ¼ pounds (910 to 1,025 g)
  lamb ribs
2 teaspoons dry mustard
1 tablespoon (9 g) garlic powder
1 tablespoon (9 g) onion powder
1 teaspoon cayenne pepper
1 teaspoon paprika
¼ teaspoon salt
¼ teaspoon freshly ground
  black pepper
¼ cup (60 ml) Worcestershire
  sauce
½ cup (120 ml) AB's BBQ Sauce or
  your favorite sauce, plus more
  for serving

EVERYONE KNOWS LAMB CHOPS and leg of lamb. If you've never had them, may I suggest you try lamb ribs? Just as with pork and beef ribs, the extra marbling of fat adds rich flavor and mouthwatering moistness.

1 Preheat the grill to 375°F (190°C). Lightly spray or brush a large heatproof baking dish with olive oil.

2 Add the ribs to the baking dish, spacing them out evenly.

3 Make a rub by whisking together the dry mustard, garlic and onion powders, cayenne, paprika, salt, and pepper in a small bowl. Rub the ribs with the mixture firmly on all sides. Add the Worcestershire sauce to the baking dish, pouring it between the ribs. Cover with foil, place the ribs in the grill, cover the grill, and cook for 1 hour.

4 Remove the ribs from the grill and flip them over with tongs. Brush them with the basting liquid in the baking dish and the barbecue sauce. Remove the foil, return them to the grill, cover the grill, and roast for 15 minutes longer. Finally, remove the ribs from the baking dish, set the dish aside, and grill the ribs on the grill grates for 10 minutes longer. Serve hot, with more barbecue sauce.

Rubbed & Grilled LAMB BREAST

SERVES 4

PREP TIME: *10 minutes, plus marinating time*
COOK TIME: *1 hour*

1 ½ pounds (680 g) boneless lamb breast
1 tablespoon (15 ml) olive oil

For the Dry Rub
1 teaspoon paprika
1 teaspoon ground cinnamon
1 teaspoon ground allspice
1 teaspoon garlic powder
1 teaspoon onion powder
1 teaspoon ground cumin
1 teaspoon salt
1 teaspoon freshly ground black pepper
2 teaspoons dried mint leaves

BEFORE GRILLING AND BARBECUE WERE FANCY things that happened in high-end big city restaurants, they were often ways for rural and small-town people to cook cheaper cuts of meat and make them taste as good as or better than the fancy cuts. One such cut is lamb breast, a fatty (but you can trim as much of the fat as you like) cut from the lamb's belly that costs a lot less than other cuts of lamb. You won't be sorry you tried it.

1 Thoroughly rinse the lamb breast and pat it dry. Rub the entire surface of the meat with the olive oil. Place the meat in a covered bowl in the refrigerator for 1 hour.

2 To make the rub, combine all the ingredients in a bowl.

3 Preheat the grill to medium heat, about 350°F (180°C). Make one side of the grill the cool side, either by turning the burners off on that side (gas grill) or moving the coals away from that side (charcoal grill).

4 Rub the lamb thoroughly with the dry rub. Transfer the lamb to the cool side, cover the grill, and let the meat cook for 40 minutes, flipping the meat over halfway through the cooking time.

5 Move the meat to the hot side of the grill and grill for 10 to 12 minutes, flipping it halfway through, until it is nicely charred.

6 Remove the lamb from the grill, let it rest for 5 to 10 minutes, then slice and serve hot.

Grilled Rosemary
LAMB CHOPS

SERVES 4 TO 8

PREP TIME: *5 minutes, plus marinating time*
COOK TIME: *18 minutes*

3 tablespoons (45 ml)
　　extra-virgin olive oil
3 cloves garlic, minced
2 tablespoons (8 g) chopped
　　fresh rosemary
Salt and freshly ground
　　black pepper
8 medium lamb loin chops

YOU DON'T NEED TO DO MUCH to make these grilled chops taste great. It's all in the ingredients—lamb from a good meat department or butcher, a good-quality olive oil, rosemary at peak freshness, and firm, fresh garlic cloves.

1　Stir together the oil, garlic, rosemary, salt, and pepper in a bowl. Coat the chops well with this marinade and cover and refrigerate for at least 1 hour and up to overnight.

2　Preheat the grill to medium-high heat, about 425°F (220°C). Create an indirect heat fire, with no coals or burners on one side.

3　Arrange the chops over this cool side of the grill and let them cook for about 10 minutes, until they have an internal temperature of about 110°F (43°C).

4　Now slide the chops over to the hot side of the grill and sear them over direct heat for 3 to 4 minutes per side, until they register 135°F (57°C) for medium-rare or 145°F (63°C) for medium. Put the chops on a platter or plates and let rest for 4 to 6 minutes. Serve hot.

FROM THE Smoker

Your Basic Down-Home
SMOKED PORK BUTT

SERVES 10

PREP TIME: 10 minutes
COOK TIME: 8 hours

½ cup (100 g) packed brown sugar
3 tablespoons (50 g) salt
2 teaspoons garlic powder
1 teaspoon onion powder
1 teaspoon freshly ground black
    pepper
1 teaspoon cayenne pepper
8 pounds (3.6 kg) pork butt roast,
    trimmed

IN MUCH OF THE SOUTH, ESPECIALLY THE CAROLINAS, pork butt is the quintessential meat for smoke-cooked barbecue. When it's not shredded and sauced up for pulled pork, it's served in slices on the plate, as here.

1 In a small bowl, mix together the brown sugar, salt, garlic powder, onion powder, pepper, and cayenne. Rub the spice mixture all over the meat and let rest for 30 minutes at room temperature.

2 Preheat the smoker to 225°F (107°C), using hardwood smoking chips (oak, hickory, or applewood).

3 Place the pork in the smoker and smoke for 4 hours without opening the smoker.

4 Remove the meat from the smoker and wrap it in a double layer of butcher paper. Place the wrapped meat back in the smoker, insert a meat thermometer in the middle, and continue to smoke until it reads 200°F (93°C), about 4 hours longer.

5 Let the meat rest for at least 30 minutes still wrapped before opening the paper, slicing, and serving with your favorite barbecue sauce.

St. Louis-Style
PORK RIBS

SERVES 3

PREP TIME: 15 minutes
COOK TIME: 2 hours and 40 minutes

½ cup (120 ml) apple juice
½ cup (120 ml) water
4 pounds (1.8 kg) St. Louis-style pork ribs, membrane removed
3 tablespoons (45 ml) grainy mustard
AB's BBQ Rub or your favorite dry rub
½ cup (112 g) unsalted butter, cubed
⅓ cup (65 g) packed brown sugar
1 cup (240 ml) barbecue sauce

PASSED DOWN THROUGH THE YEARS, this culinary gem pays tribute, again, to my grandfather, who first introduced me to pork ribs during my youth. Imagine trimmed ribs, seasoned with a blend of a spice rub, mustard, and brown sugar that brings together sweet, smoky, and a touch of heat. The smoker comes to life, infusing the ribs with flavors that tell a story of barbecue traditions.

1 Preheat the smoker to 275°F (140°C), using hardwood smoking chips (hickory, oak, or applewood).

2 Mix the apple juice and water together in a spray bottle and set it aside.

3 Coat the ribs in the mustard and season generously with the dry rub. Place the seasoned ribs in the smoker, bone-side down, with space between them for smoke circulation. Close the lid and smoke the ribs for 1 hour, maintaining a consistent temperature of 275°F (140°C). Spritz them with the apple juice mixture.

4 Lay down a double layer of foil and arrange the butter cubes and brown sugar in the center, approximately the size of the ribs. Place the ribs on the foil and wrap them up tightly, crimping the edges to create a leak-proof packet.

5 Place the ribs back in the smoker and smoke until the meat is tender enough to pull away from the bone, about 1½ hours longer.

6 Unwrap the ribs, brush with the barbecue sauce, and smoke for 10 minutes longer, until the sauce becomes sticky.

7 Remove the ribs from the smoker and allow them to rest for 10 minutes before slicing. Enjoy!

Smoked
GLAZED HAM

SERVES 10

PREP TIME: 15 minutes
COOK TIME: 4 hours

One 7-pound (3.2 kg) cooked,
   bone-in, spiral-cut ham
¾ cup (180 ml) orange juice
⅓ cup (65 g) packed brown sugar
⅓ cup (110 g) honey
¾ teaspoon ground cinnamon
½ teaspoon ground cloves
¼ teaspoon ground nutmeg
1 tablespoon (8 g) cornstarch
1 tablespoon (15 ml) water

HANDS-DOWN THIS IS THE BEST WAY TO PREPARE a spiral-cut ham, as far as I'm concerned. The deep flavor of the wood smoke does two things here. It infuses the ham meat with a rustic country flavor and it gives a tasty woodsy accent to the glaze, making the glaze a little less sweet and a lot more flavorful.

1 Preheat the smoker to 225°F (107°C), using hardwood smoking chips (hickory, oak, or applewood).

2 Place the ham, cut-side down, in the smoker and smoke for 2 hours.

3 While the ham is smoking, heat the orange juice, brown sugar, honey, cinnamon, cloves, and nutmeg in a medium saucepan over medium-high heat. Bring the mixture to a gentle boil, reduce the heat to low, and simmer for 4 minutes.

4 In a cup, mix the cornstarch and water until blended and pour it into the orange juice mixture, whisking constantly until the glaze thickens, about 1 minute. Remove the glaze from the heat and set aside.

5 Increase the smoker temperature to 325°F (170°C) and brush the glaze generously on the ham.

6 Continue smoking the ham, and brushing on glaze, until it reaches an internal temperature of 140°F (60°C), about 2 hours. Let the ham rest for 15 minutes before slicing.

Pork Belly
BURNT ENDS

SERVES 6

PREP TIME: 15 minutes
COOK TIME: 4 ½ hours

1 tablespoon (12 g) brown sugar
2 teaspoons chili powder
1 teaspoon smoked paprika
1 teaspoon garlic powder
1 teaspoon ground cumin
1 teaspoon salt
½ teaspoon freshly ground black pepper
3 pounds (1,365 g) pork belly, cut into 1½-inch (3.8 cm) cubes
2 tablespoons (30 ml) olive oil
⅔ cup (160 ml) barbecue sauce of choice
3 tablespoons (42 g) unsalted butter, melted

I AM A MAN OF TRADITION, and as such I don't often hop on board the latest food trend. I make an exception for pork belly, which used to be hard to find in stores but has lately become super trendy and popular. It's a fattier and more flavor-packed cut of pork than chops or tenderloins, and if you have not had it you'll be sure to enjoy discovering it. In fact, the meat has always been valued in traditional barbecue circles; it's only lately been discovered by the rest of the world.

1 Preheat the smoker to 250°F (120°C), using hardwood smoking chips (hickory, oak, or applewood).

2 In a small bowl, mix together the brown sugar, chili powder, smoked paprika, garlic powder, cumin, salt, and pepper.

3 Place the pork belly in a large bowl and toss with the oil. Add the spice mixture and toss to coat the pork thoroughly. Place the seasoned pork belly in the smoker, close the lid, and smoke until the cubes are a dark reddish color, about 2 ½ hours.

4 In a small bowl, whisk the barbecue sauce and butter.

5 Transfer the pork to a large disposable aluminum roasting pan and add the barbecue sauce mixture, tossing to coat.

6 Cover the pan with foil, return it to the smoker, and cook for 2 hours longer, or until the pork has an internal temperature of 250°F (120°C). Allow the pork to rest for 10 minutes before serving.

CHAPTER

Four

FIRE-KISSED
FISH & SHELLFISH

Foil-Pack GRILLED SHRIMP BOIL

SERVES 4

PREP TIME: 20 minutes
COOK TIME: 16 minutes

2 quarts (1.8 L) water
1 pound (455 g) baby or
    fingerling potatoes, cut into
    1-inch (2.5 cm) cubes
2 ears fresh corn, cut or broken into
    2-inch (5 cm) rounds
1 ½ pounds (680 g) fresh medium
    or large uncooked shrimp,
    peeled and deveined
12 ounces (340 g) andouille
    smoked sausage, cut into 2-inch
    (5 cm) rounds
¼ cup chopped onion
4 cloves garlic, minced
¼ cup (56 g) unsalted butter,
    melted
1 teaspoon salt
½ teaspoon freshly ground black
    pepper
2 tablespoons (12 g) Old Bay
    Seasoning (preferably) or other
    Louisiana-style seasoning
    mixture for seafood
Chopped fresh parsley, for garnish
Lemon wedges or slices, for garnish

LIKE A LOUISIANA SHRIMP BOIL (or a Midwestern fish boil), except from the grill and not from a big cauldron.

1 Preheat the grill to 400°F (200°C). Have ready four heavy-duty aluminum foil sheets, about 12 inches (30.5 cm) square.

2 Add the water to a stockpot and bring to a boil over high heat on the stovetop. Add the potatoes and corn, reduce the heat to a simmer, and cook for 10 minutes, until soft but not mushy. Remove from the heat and drain.

3 In a large bowl, gently stir together the shrimp, sausage, onion, garlic, potatoes, and corn. Pour the butter over the mixture and season with the salt, pepper, and Old Bay Seasoning. Stir again to combine well. Place one-fourth of this mixture in the center of each aluminum foil sheet. Wrap the foil securely around each packet, sealing well.

4 Transfer the packets to the grill and cook for 7 to 8 minutes. Flip them over and cook for 7 to 8 minutes longer. Open the packets carefully, garnish with parsley and lemon, and serve hot.

Sweet & Hot
BARBECUE GRILLED SHRIMP

SERVES 2

PREP TIME: 15 minutes
COOK TIME: 8 minutes

⅓ cup (80 ml) barbecue sauce

¼ cup (80 g) honey

2 tablespoons (30 ml) chili sauce

2 teaspoons minced garlic

1 pound (455 g) large (31/35 count) tail-on shrimp, peeled and deveined

8 metal skewers or wooden skewers soaked in water for 30 minutes

2 tablespoons (30 ml) olive oil

Salt and freshly ground black pepper

Chopped scallion, for garnish

PART OF THE FUN OF GRILLING is that you can walk away from the grill and do something else as the food cooks. Resist this temptation when you are grilling shrimp, however: Shrimp can get tough and over-cooked pretty quickly. On that note, if you can't find large shrimp and have to substitute medium shrimp, reduce the cooking time by half.

1 Preheat the grill to medium heat, about 350°F (180°C).

2 In a medium bowl, mix the barbecue sauce, honey, chili sauce, and garlic. Reserve half the sauce for serving.

3 Thread the shrimp onto the skewers, dividing them evenly and leaving a little space between them for even cooking. Brush the shrimp with the oil and season with salt and pepper.

4 Grill the shrimp until opaque and lightly charred, turning every 2 min-utes, around 8 minutes total time. Brush the shrimp with the barbecue sauce while grilling.

5 Serve garnished with scallions and the reserved sauce for dipping.

Creole
Garlic Butter
GRILLED SHRIMP SKEWERS

SERVES 6

PREP TIME: 20 minutes
COOK TIME: 8 minutes

½ cup (112 g) unsalted butter, melted

Juice of 1 lemon

1 tablespoon (4 g) chopped fresh curly parsley

1 tablespoon (6 g) Creole seasoning

2 teaspoons minced garlic

2 pounds (910 g) large (31/35 count) tail-on shrimp, peeled and deveined

6 metal skewers or wooden skewers soaked in water for 30 minutes

YOU CAN MAKE YOUR OWN CREOLE SEASONING MIX—the ingredients are dried thyme, paprika, garlic powder, onion powder, and chili powder—but there are so many good brands for sale in the supermarket that you don't have to. The Gulf Coast of Louisiana is a famous shrimp fishery and so it makes sense that Creole Louisianians would create a spice mix that tastes terrific on shrimp. Add some garlic butter and lemon and you're all set.

1 Preheat the grill to medium heat, about 350°F (180°C).

2 In a medium bowl, mix together the butter, lemon juice, parsley, seasoning, and garlic. Reserve half the sauce for basting.

3 Add the shrimp to the remaining butter mixture, tossing to coat. Thread the shrimp onto the skewers, dividing them evenly and leaving a little space between them for even cooking.

4 Grill the shrimp until opaque and lightly charred, turning once, around 8 minutes total time. Brush the shrimp with the reserved butter mixture while grilling. Serve.

Grilled
LOBSTERS

SERVES 2

PREP TIME: *30 minutes*
COOK TIME: *12 minutes*

Two 1 ½-pound (680 g) whole
    lobsters
2 tablespoons (30 ml) olive oil
Salt and freshly ground black
    pepper
½ cup (112 g) unsalted butter
1 tablespoon (8 g) minced garlic
Juice of ½ lemon
1 tablespoon (4 g) chopped fresh
    curly parsley, plus more for
    garnish

NOTHING COULD BE MORE STRAIGHTFORWARD than this process—a quick drizzle of olive oil, a sprinkle of salt and pepper, and a baste of lemony garlic butter. The sizzle and scent are captivating as the lobsters cook to tender perfection.

1 Preheat the grill to medium heat, about 350°F (180°C).

2 Rinse the lobsters under cold water and pat them dry with paper towels. Split the lobsters lengthwise using shears, scoop out and discard the yellow-green innards, and snap off and crack the claws. Drizzle the lobster meat with the oil and season with salt and pepper.

3 In a small saucepan, melt the butter over low heat and stir in the garlic and lemon juice. Cook for 2 minutes, remove the butter mixture from the heat, stir in the parsley, and set aside.

4 Place the lobster halves and claws on the grill, flesh-side down. Grill until the flesh becomes opaque, about 5 minutes.

5 Flip the lobster halves and claws over and baste the flesh with the garlic butter sauce. Grill, basting with the sauce, until the flesh is cooked and the internal temperature is 140°F (60°C), about 5 minutes.

6 Transfer the lobster halves and claws to a serving platter and garnish with chopped parsley.

Grilled
MAHI MAHI

SERVES 2

PREP TIME: *10 minutes*
COOK TIME: *10 minutes*

½ teaspoon garlic powder
½ teaspoon smoked paprika
½ teaspoon salt
¼ teaspoon freshly ground black
  pepper
Two 6-ounce (168 g) skin-on mahi
  mahi fillets
1 tablespoon (15 ml) olive oil
2 tablespoons (28 g) unsalted
  butter, melted
Chopped fresh dill, for garnish
Lemon wedges or slices, for garnish

IF MAHI MAHI IS HARD TO FIND where you live, you can substitute another firm but flaky white fish, such as snapper, grouper, haddock, or cod.

1 Preheat the grill to medium-high heat, about 400°F (200°C). Clean the grates thoroughly and lightly oil them.

2 In a small bowl, mix together the garlic powder, paprika, salt, and pepper.

3 Brush the fillets all over with the olive oil and season with the spice mixture. Arrange the fish, flesh-side down, on the grill and grill until the fillets reach an internal temperature of 165°F (74°C), turning once, about 10 minutes total.

4 Remove the fish from the grill and brush the fillets with the butter. Serve topped with chopped dill and lemon wedges or slices.

Brown Sugar GRILLED SALMON

SERVES 4

PREP TIME: *10 minutes*
COOK TIME: *12 minutes*

¼ cup (50 g) brown sugar
1 tablespoon (2 g) dried parsley
2 teaspoons garlic powder
2 teaspoons paprika
1 teaspoon salt
½ teaspoon freshly ground
   black pepper
Four 5-ounce (140 g) skin-on
   salmon fillets, about 1 inch
   (2.5 cm) thick
Olive oil, as needed

SWEET AND SAVORY MEET IN THIS QUICK but fancy dinner, one of my go-to choices when I have company over. Fresh salmon fillets with a caramelized brown sugar glaze, kissed by the flavor of smoke from the grill, are my idea of perfection.

1 Preheat the grill to high heat, about 450°F (230°C). Clean the grates thoroughly and lightly oil them.

2 In a small bowl, mix together the brown sugar, parsley, garlic powder, paprika, salt, and pepper.

3 Pat the salmon dry with paper towels, brush them all over with olive oil, and season with the spice mixture. Arrange the fish, skin-side down, on the grill, close the lid, and grill until they reach an internal temperature of 145°F (63°C), turning once, 10 to 12 minutes total. Remove the fish from the grill and serve.

Louisiana
HONEY-GRILLED SALMON

SERVES 4

PREP TIME: 10 minutes
COOK TIME: 18 minutes

For the Cajun Seasoning
2 teaspoons garlic powder
1 teaspoon onion powder
2 teaspoons paprika, preferably smoked
1 teaspoon cayenne pepper
2 teaspoons dried Italian seasoning or dried parsley
1 teaspoon freshly cracked black pepper
1 teaspoon salt
1 teaspoon red pepper flakes
¼ cup (56 g) unsalted butter, at room temperature
2 tablespoons (40 g) honey

4 medium to large salmon fillets, trimmed of skin
Olive oil
Salt and freshly ground black pepper
4 to 8 sprigs fresh parsley

THERE ARE MANY BRANDS OF CAJUN SEASONING available in stores just about anywhere. Here we will make our own that's just as good—or even better! We will use about 2 tablespoons (12 g) here; store the extra seasoning mixture in a cool, dry place.

1   Preheat the grill to 350°F (180°C).

2   To make the Cajun seasoning, in a bowl, combine the garlic powder, onion powder, paprika, cayenne, Italian seasoning, pepper, salt, and red pepper flakes and set aside. Whip the butter in a second bowl with a hand mixer or a whisk until it gets light and airy. Whip in the honey. Add 2 tablespoons (12 g) of the dry seasoning mixture and stir into the butter and honey.

3   Meanwhile, pat the salmon fillets dry with paper towels and then coat them with olive oil on all sides.

4   Transfer the salmon to the grill and cook for about 8 minutes on each side (or 5 or 6 minutes if the fillets are on the thin side), until the fish is no longer translucent and flakes with a fork.

5   Spoon half the seasoned honey-butter evenly over the top of the salmon fillets, flip them over, and spoon the remaining honey-butter over the other side. Remove the fish from the grill, garnish with the parsley, and serve hot.

Blackened
GRILLED COD

SERVES 4

PREP TIME: *5 minutes*
COOK TIME: *12 minutes*

Four 4- to 6-ounce (112 to 168 g)
    cod fillets
2 tablespoons (30 ml) olive oil
¾ teaspoon salt
½ teaspoon freshly ground
    black pepper
2 tablespoons (12 g) blackened
    seasoning

COD HAS A UNIQUE FLAVOR but it is not always available in every market. Tilapia, haddock, bass, and sea bass are all good substitutes for this recipe. All of the makers of Cajun and Creole seasoning mixes also make "blackened seasoning," and it is very easy to find nowadays.

1   Let the cod fillets come to room temperature for 15 to 20 minutes.

2   Meanwhile, preheat the grill to medium-high heat, about 375°F (190°C), with all the coals, or burners, lit on one side of the grill.

3   Pat the fillets dry with a paper towel and coat them on all sides with the olive oil. Season the fillets on all sides with the salt, pepper, and blackened seasoning.

4   Place the cod on the cool side of the grill and cook for 3 to 4 minutes on each side, until the fish is no longer translucent and flakes easily with a fork. Transfer it gently to the hot side of the grill and let it sear lightly for 2 minutes. Remove from the grill, let rest for 5 minutes, and serve hot.

Grilled
LIME-BASIL HALIBUT

SERVES 4

PREP TIME: 10 minutes, plus
marinating time
COOK TIME: 12 minutes

¼ cup (60 ml) extra-virgin olive oil
¼ cup (60 ml) fresh lime juice,
  from about 2 limes
3 cloves garlic, minced
1 teaspoon lime zest
1 ½ tablespoons (23 ml) bottled hot
  sauce
¼ cup (16 g) minced fresh basil
1 tablespoon (8 g) bottled capers
4 halibut fillets or steaks, about
  6 ounces (168 g) each
½ teaspoon salt
½ teaspoon freshly ground
  black pepper

HALIBUT HAS GOTTEN A LITTLE PRICEY in recent years. Save this showstopper recipe for a fancy dinner for company.

1 In a blender or food processor, or in a bowl with a whisk, combine the olive oil, lime juice, garlic, lime zest, and hot sauce. Transfer to a bowl and stir in the basil and capers.

2 Place the fish in a large glass baking dish in one layer. Cover with half of the marinade and cover tightly with plastic wrap. Set aside and reserve the other half of the marinade. Let the fish marinate in the refrigerator for 30 minutes—but no more (because the acid in the lime will begin breaking down the fish if they are in contact too long). Turn the fillets once or twice so that their entire surface is exposed to the marinade.

3 Preheat the grill to high heat, about 450°F (230°C).

4 Pat any excess marinade off of the fillets. Season them with the salt and pepper. Transfer to the hot grill and grill for 4 to 6 minutes per side, depending on their thickness.

5 Remove from the grill and let the fish rest for 5 minutes. Transfer to plates and top each serving with the reserved marinade. Serve hot.

Grilled
WHOLE RED
SNAPPER

SERVES 4

PREP TIME: 15 minutes, plus marinating time
COOK TIME: 25 minutes

3 tablespoons (12 g) fresh thyme leaves

2 tablespoons minced (8 g) fresh basil

¼ cup (16 g) minced fresh parsley

4 cloves garlic, minced

2 tablespoons (30 ml) olive oil

1 tablespoon (15 ml) fresh lemon juice

½ teaspoon salt

¼ teaspoon white pepper

½ teaspoon powdered chicken bouillon (optional)

1 whole red snapper, 1 to 1 ½ pounds (455 to 680 g), cleaned, gutted, and scaled

IT'S NOT TO EVERYONE'S TASTE, but I happen to love the sight of a whole fish, cooked to perfection and seasoned well, on a platter in the middle of the table. And you can't do much better than red snapper.

1 Stir together the thyme, basil, parsley, and garlic in a bowl. Add the olive oil, lemon juice, salt, white pepper, and powdered bouillon (if using) and stir to combine well. Set aside.

2 Trim the fins off the fish with a sharp knife or kitchen shears. Rinse the fish and pat it dry.

3 Use a sharp paring knife to cut four to six diagonal slits, each about ½ inch (1.3 cm) deep, on both sides of the snapper. Rub half of the herb-and-garlic mixture over the fish and into the slits. Rub some of the mixture into the fish's gutted cavity. Transfer the fish to a large glass baking dish lined with parchment paper. Cover with plastic wrap and let it marinate at room temperature for 20 minutes.

4 Meanwhile, preheat the grill to medium-high heat, about 375°F (190°C).

5 Remove the fish from the glass dish and transfer it to the grill. Grill for 20 minutes, flipping the fish once at the halfway point. Brush the fish a few times with additional olive oil.

6 Briefly raise the heat to high, about 450°F (230°C) and grill the fish 4 to 5 more minutes, so that it sears and chars a little, but take care not to burn the fish. You just want a light charring. Remove the fish from the grill and let it rest for 5 to 10 minutes. Slice into portions and serve hot.

Candied
SMOKED SALMON BITES

SERVES 4

PREP TIME: *15 minutes, plus marinating time*
COOK TIME: *6 hours*

1 ½ cups (360 ml) water
1 cup (200 g) packed brown sugar
¾ cup (240 g) honey
¼ cup (50 g) salt
One 4-pound (1.8 kg) skinless, boneless salmon side, cut into 1-inch (2.5 cm) cubes

THEY'RE TIME-CONSUMING, FOR SURE, but if you're planning a day or evening with your smoker, these delectable cubes really don't take much effort. During the long smoking time the brown sugar and honey flavors are infused into the fish, so that by the end the coating is not as sugary sweet as you might expect.

1 In a large bowl, whisk together the water, brown sugar, honey, and salt until the sugar is dissolved. Add the salmon cubes, cover, and refrigerate for at least 4 hours and up to overnight. Remove the salmon from the marinade, reserving the marinade.

2 Preheat the smoker to 200°F (93°C), using hardwood smoking chips (hickory, oak, or applewood). Line the smoker grates with foil.

3   Arrange the salmon cubes on the foil with a little space between them to ensure even smoking. Smoke the salmon for 1 hour.

4 While the salmon is smoking, pour the marinade into a large saucepan and bring it to a boil over medium-high heat. Decrease the heat to low and simmer until the liquid reduces to a thicker glaze, skimming off any film that forms on the surface, about 15 minutes. Remove the glaze from the heat and set aside.

5 After 1 hour of smoking, flip the salmon cubes and brush them with the glaze. Continue smoking the fish, flipping and brushing every hour, until the cubes are lightly caramelized and reach an internal temperature of 160°F (71°C), about 5 hours. Serve.

CHAPTER

Five

CHEESE & VEGGIE
SIDES AND MAINS

Smoked
MAC & CHEESE

SERVES 4

PREP TIME: 15 minutes
COOK TIME: 1 hour and 10 minutes

12 ounces (340 g) large elbow macaroni

8 thick-cut slices bacon

½ cup (50 g) panko

2 tablespoons (28 g) unsalted butter

2 tablespoons (16 g) all-purpose flour

2 cups (480 ml) heavy (whipping) cream

1 cup (240 ml) sour cream

12 ounces (340 g) shredded extra-sharp Cheddar cheese

8 ounces (227 g) shredded Gouda cheese

8 ounces (227 g) shredded Monterey cheese

2 tablespoons (12 g) Creole seasoning

SMOKED MAC & CHEESE, Y'ALL! Here is a recipe that holds a special place in my heart. You see, it was my grandma who led me into the world of cooking. And this dish? This dish was one of the first steps on that path. Back then, I was a newbie in the kitchen, eager to learn and make my mark. Grandma, with her apron on and wisdom in her eyes, guided me through the process. As I ventured further into cooking, this mac & cheese remained my go-to, a signature dish of mine that brought smiles and comfort to my family. It was a nod to my grandma's teachings, a way of keeping her spirit alive in the kitchen. And you know what? It's still a hit today.

1 Preheat your smoker or grill to medium heat, about 350°F (180°C). Lightly coat a 9 by 13-inch (23 by 33 cm) baking dish or cast-iron skillet with nonstick cooking spray.

2 In a large pot of salted water, cook the elbow macaroni according to the package instructions until al dente, about 12 minutes. Drain the macaroni in a strainer and set aside.

3 In a large skillet over medium-high heat, cook the bacon until crispy, about 7 minutes. Transfer the bacon to a plate and reserve the bacon fat.

4 When the bacon is cool, chop it into small pieces and transfer them to a small bowl. Add the panko to the bacon and toss to coat; set the mixture aside.

5 In a large saucepan over medium heat, melt the butter with the reserved bacon fat. Whisk in the flour and cook for 1 to 2 minutes, whisking constantly, until the mixture forms a smooth paste. Gradually whisk in the cream and cook the sauce until it thickens and becomes creamy, 5 to 7 minutes longer. Whisk in the sour cream until combined. Reduce the heat to low and add the shredded cheeses to the sauce, stirring until they are completely melted and the sauce is smooth. Stir in the cooked macaroni and Creole seasoning and adjust the seasonings to suit your taste.

CONTINUED ➡

6 Add the macaroni and cheese to the prepared baking dish and spread in an even layer. Sprinkle the bacon mixture over the mac & cheese and place the dish on the smoker. Smoke for approximately 40 minutes until bubbly and golden. Serve.

7 Refrigerate any leftovers in a covered dish for up to 5 days.

Grilled
CHEESY BLOOMING ONION

SERVES 2

PREP TIME: 15 minutes
COOK TIME: 30 minutes

1 large sweet onion, peeled
1 teaspoon olive oil
Salt and freshly ground black pepper
¼ cup (30 g) shredded sharp Cheddar cheese
2 tablespoons (15 g) shredded Gruyère or mozzarella cheese
Sriracha or your favorite steak sauce

IN NORTH AMERICA, THE THREE MOST COMMON VARIETIES of sweet onions are Walla Walla, Vidalia, and Texas Sweet, but they go by other names around the world. This grilled onion treat isn't bad made with an ordinary yellow onion, but it's much better, I think, if you make sure you get your hands on a bona fide sweet onion. Fortunately, most supermarkets now have them year-round.

1 Preheat the grill to medium-high heat, about 400°F (200°C).

2 Place the peeled onion base-side down on a cutting board and, starting at the top, cut it into 8 wedges, stopping before cutting all the way through. The base should be left intact.

3 Place the onion on a 12-inch (30.5 cm) square piece of foil and gently open the wedges so the onion resembles a flower. Drizzle the onion with the olive oil and season with salt and pepper. Sprinkle the cheeses over the onion, making sure the shreds fall between the "petals."

4 Wrap the foil around the onion and grill the package until the onion is tender, about 30 minutes. Serve immediately drizzled with sriracha.

Grilled
ASPARAGUS

SERVES 4

PREP TIME: 5 minutes
COOK TIME: 5 minutes

1 pound (455 g) asparagus, woody
    ends removed
1 tablespoon (15 ml) olive oil
Salt and freshly ground black
    pepper
1 tablespoon (14 g) unsalted butter

YOU CAN SERVE THESE SMOKY, FLAME-KISSED SPEARS
alongside any grilled main course. I especially like them next to a fish or
shellfish dish or a well-grilled steak.

1 Preheat the grill to medium-high heat, about 400°F (200°C).

2 Spread the asparagus in a 9 by 13-inch (23 by 33 cm) baking dish and
   add the olive oil, tossing to coat. Season with salt and pepper.

3 Remove the asparagus from the baking dish and grill them until lightly
   charred and tender-crisp, turning once, about 5 minutes.

4 Arrange the spears on a serving plate, top with the butter, and serve.

Grilled
ROMAINE

SERVES 4

PREP TIME: 10 minutes
COOK TIME: 6 minutes

2 heads romaine, halved lengthwise
1 ½ tablespoons (23 ml) olive oil
Salt and freshly ground black
    pepper
1 lemon, halved
½ cup (60 g) grated Asiago or
    Parmesan cheese
1 tablespoon (4 g) chopped
    fresh basil

THE FIRMNESS OF ROMAINE LEAVES MEANS they hold up well on the grill, which other lettuces will not do. Blue cheese or Gorgonzola is a worthy alternative to the cheeses named in the recipe, if by chance you are a fan of them.

1 Preheat the grill to medium-high heat, about 400°F (200°C).

2 Brush the lettuce halves with the olive oil and season with salt and pepper.

3 Grill the lettuce halves, cut-side down, until they have nice grill marks, about 6 minutes, turning them halfway through.

4 Remove the halves from the grill to serving plates and top with a squeeze of fresh lemon juice, Asiago or Parmesan cheese, and basil.

Foil-Pack GRILLED PEPPERS & ZUCCHINI

SERVES 4

PREP TIME: 10 minutes
COOK TIME: 12 minutes

4 bell peppers (multicolored), seeded and julienned
2 zucchini, cut into ¼-inch (6 mm) rounds
1 ½ tablespoons (21 g) unsalted butter
½ teaspoon dried thyme
Salt and freshly ground black pepper

GREEN, RED, YELLOW, ORANGE, PURPLE, and more—there sure are a lot of choices available when you shop for bell peppers these days. Omit the green ones if you want a sweeter mix. Use mostly red ones, add a little oregano, and drizzle the grilled veggies with some olive oil at the end if you want a Mediterranean blend. Go with four zucchini and two peppers if your garden just yielded a few bushels of zucchini. In short, tailor this recipe to your tastes and to what is available.

1 Preheat the grill to medium heat, about 350°F (180°C).

2 Lay out a double layer of aluminum foil sheets, about 12 inches (30.5 cm) square. Arrange the peppers and zucchini in the middle of the foil, dot with the butter, sprinkle with the thyme, and season with salt and pepper. Fold the foil up to create a sealed packet.

3 Place the packet on the grill, close the grill, and cook until the vegetables are tender-crisp, shaking the packet halfway through, about 12 minutes in total. Open the foil carefully and serve.

Grilled
MEXICAN STREET CORN (ELOTE) SKILLET

SERVES 4

PREP TIME: 15 minutes, plus soaking time
COOK TIME: 17 minutes

7 ears fresh corn, silks removed, husk on
¼ cup (60 ml) sour cream
¼ cup (30 g) grated cotija cheese
2 tablespoons (30 ml) mayonnaise
3 tablespoons (3 g) chopped fresh cilantro
1 tablespoon (6 g) chipotle chili powder
Juice and zest of 1 lime
½ teaspoon minced garlic
Salt and freshly ground black pepper

COTIJA CHEESE CAN BE FOUND IN the Mexican or Hispanic sections of most supermarkets these days. Another Mexican cheese, queso fresco, or feta cheese is a substitute that works well. If you cannot find chipotle powder, use regular chili powder or minced canned chipotles.

1 Soak the corn in cold water for 30 minutes. Drain.

2 Preheat the grill to high heat, about 450°F (230°C).

3 Grill the corn until it is charred on all sides, 10 to 12 minutes. Remove the corn ears from the grill and let them sit until cool enough to handle. Husk the ears and cut the kernels off with a sharp knife into a medium bowl.

4 Place a cast-iron skillet on the grill. Add the corn kernels, sour cream, cotija cheese, mayonnaise, cilantro, chili powder, lime juice, lime zest, and garlic to the hot skillet and cook, stirring occasionally, until heated through and creamy, about 5 minutes. Season with salt and pepper and serve.

Grilled
DOUBLE POTATO SALAD

SERVES 4

PREP TIME: 15 minutes
COOK TIME: 6 to 8 minutes

5 large potatoes, cut into ¾-inch
   (2 cm) slices
1 sweet potato, peeled and cut into
   ¾-inch (2 cm) slices
1 small sweet onion, cut into ¾-inch
   (2 cm) slices
1 tablespoon (15 ml) olive oil
⅓ cup (80 ml) mayonnaise
1 tablespoon (15 ml) Dijon mustard
2 teaspoons garlic powder
¼ teaspoon paprika
Salt and freshly ground black
   pepper
2 tablespoons (8 g) chopped
   fresh parsley, for garnish

CAN'T DECIDE BETWEEN SWEET POTATOES AND regular potatoes? Sometimes I can't decide either. That's when I grill up both kinds and serve them together in this substantial salad.

1 Preheat the grill to medium-high heat, about 400°F (200°C).

2 In a medium bowl, toss the potato, sweet potato, and onion slices with the olive oil.

3 Arrange the vegetable slices on the grill and cook, turning, until they are just cooked through and lightly charred, 6 to 8 minutes total. Transfer the slices to a medium bowl and set aside to cool.

4 In a separate medium bowl, whisk together the mayonnaise, mustard, garlic powder, and paprika. When the vegetables are cool enough to handle, cut them into large chunks and add to the mayonnaise mixture. Toss to combine and season to taste with salt and pepper. Garnish with the parsley and serve.

Southern
POTATO
SALAD

SERVES 6

PREP TIME: 15 minutes, plus
chilling time
COOK TIME: 15 minutes

6 russet potatoes, peeled and cut
    into 1-inch (2.5 cm) chunks
5 large eggs
1 onion, finely chopped
1 cup (240 ml) mayonnaise
½ cup (120 g) sweet relish
2 tablespoons (30 ml) yellow
    mustard
1 teaspoon smoked paprika
Salt and freshly ground black
    pepper
Level Up A Rub (optional)

THERE'S NO GRILLING HERE. But there is so much tradition in serving a Southern-style potato salad as part of a grilled dinner that it would be a crime to omit this salad from a book on grilling.

1 Place the potatoes in a large saucepan with enough cold water to cover them by 2 inches (5 cm). Bring the water to a boil over high heat and cook the potatoes until fork-tender, about 15 minutes.

2 While the potatoes are cooking, place the eggs in a small saucepan and cover them with 2 inches (5 cm) of cold water. Bring the water to a boil over high heat and cook the eggs for 2 minutes. Remove the saucepan from the heat, drain, and refill the saucepan with cold water. Set the eggs aside.

3 Drain the potatoes and transfer them to a large bowl.

4 Peel and chop the eggs and add them to the potatoes along with the mayonnaise, relish, mustard, and paprika. Stir well to combine. Season with salt, pepper, and Level Up A Rub (if using).

5 Cover the salad and refrigerate for at least 2 hours to let the flavors mellow. Serve.

Grilled
SWEET POTATOES

SERVES 4

PREP TIME: 10 minutes
COOK TIME: 12 minutes

2 pounds (910 g) sweet potatoes,
    cut lengthwise into ¼-inch
    (6 mm) thick slices
¼ cup (60 ml) olive oil
Salt
Parsley (optional), for garnish

I WON'T GET INTO THE SWEET POTATO VERSUS yam debate. Suffice it to say that either one would be fine in this straightforward, simple recipe.

1 Preheat the grill to high heat, about 450°F (230°C).

2 In a medium bowl, toss the sweet potato slices with the oil and season with salt.

3 Arrange the sweet potato slices on the grill and cook until they are tender and lightly charred, about 12 minutes, turning halfway through. Serve, garnished with parsley if you like.

Bourbon Bacon
GRILLED BAKED BEANS

SERVES 4

PREP TIME: 10 minutes
COOK TIME: 39 minutes

8 ounces (227 g) bacon, chopped
1 small onion, chopped
One 16 ½-ounce (470 g) can
    baked beans
¼ cup (60 ml) bourbon
3 tablespoons (36 g) packed
    brown sugar
1 tablespoon (15 ml) Dijon
    mustard
1 teaspoon minced garlic
1 teaspoon chipotle chili powder
¼ teaspoon ground cumin
Pinch of cayenne pepper
Salt and freshly ground black
    pepper

FOR THE TEETOTALERS, substitute 2 tablespoons (30 ml) of balsamic vinegar for the bourbon and you'll get some of the same richness and punch. If your canned baked beans are a particularly sugary brand, omit 1 tablespoon (12 g) of the brown sugar in the recipe to compensate for that.

1 Preheat the grill to medium heat, about 350°F (180°C). Turn off half the burners.

2 Place a 9-inch (23 cm) cast-iron skillet on the hot side of the grill and cook the bacon until it releases the fat, about 3 minutes.

3 Add the onion and continue to cook, stirring frequently, until the bacon is crispy and the onion is browned, about 6 minutes.

4 Transfer the skillet to the cool side and stir in the beans, bourbon, brown sugar, mustard, garlic, chili powder, cumin, salt, pepper, and cayenne.

5 Close the lid on the grill and let the beans cook on the cool side, stirring occasionally, until heated through, thickened, and bubbly, about 30 minutes. Serve.

Grilled
TOMATO &
RED PEPPER
SOUP

SERVES 4

PREP TIME: *25 minutes*
COOK TIME: *7 minutes*

4 tablespoons (60 ml) olive oil
1 pound (455 g) red bell peppers,
  seeded and halved
1 large sweet onion, cut into
  ½-inch (1.3 cm) slices
2 large cloves garlic
2 pounds (910 g) large ripe
  tomatoes, stemmed and halved
½ cup (30 g) fresh basil leaves
1 teaspoon balsamic vinegar
1 cup (240 ml) chicken or
  vegetable broth, plus more
  as needed
Salt and freshly ground black
  pepper
Shredded Asiago cheese,
  for serving

TOMATOES ARE ALWAYS AT THEIR BEST when in season, which is in the hot months of late summer. But what about the ten months of the year that are outside that short two-month window? Here's a suggestion: Put out-of-season tomatoes on the grill. The hot flames will caramelize the exposed part of the tomatoes and amplify their natural sugar and flavor. Eat grilled tomatoes straight up with a little salt, or dressed with oil and vinegar, or, for something really good, in this very hearty tomato and pepper soup.

1 Preheat the grill to medium heat, about 350°F (180°C). Thoroughly clean the grates and oil them well.

2 In a medium bowl, toss 2 tablespoons (30 ml) of the oil with the bell peppers, onion, and garlic, keeping the onion slices as intact as possible.

3 Brush the cut side of the tomatoes with 2 tablespoons (30 ml) of the oil and place them cut-side down on the grill. Arrange the bell peppers (skin-side down), onion, and garlic on the grill as well. (You might need to use a grill basket for the garlic.)

4 Close the lid and cook until the tomato skins loosen and all the vegetables soften and get lightly charred, about 7 minutes. Turn the peppers and onion at least once.

5 Remove the vegetables to a large bowl, keeping the tomatoes to one side, and let them cool for 10 minutes.

6 Place a fine-mesh sieve over a medium bowl and, working over the bowl to catch the juice, use your hands to skin and seed the tomatoes, placing the flesh in a blender as you go.

7 Skin the peppers and place them, the onion, garlic, basil, balsamic vinegar, and reserved tomato juices in the blender with the tomatoes. Blend until smooth, adding enough broth to achieve the desired consistency.

8 Pour the soup into a large saucepan and heat over medium-low heat until piping hot.

9 Season with salt and pepper and serve topped with Asiago cheese.

Grill-Roasted
CABBAGE WITH BACON

SERVES 4

PREP TIME: 10 minutes
COOK TIME: 40 minutes

1 pound (455 g) bacon, chopped
1 small cabbage, quartered
    lengthwise
1 teaspoon olive oil
Juice of ¼ lemon
1 teaspoon soy sauce
Freshly ground black pepper

Y'ALL KNOW I LIKE MY FRIED CABBAGE. Well, this roasted cabbage and bacon from the grill is my favorite for outdoor cooking. You've got to put this out on the table and see how fast it goes!

1 Preheat the grill to medium heat, about 350°F (180°C).

2 Place a large ovenproof skillet over medium-high heat on the stovetop and cook the bacon until crispy, about 10 minutes. Transfer the bacon bits with a slotted spoon to a paper towel–lined plate and set aside.

3 Wipe the skillet out and arrange the cabbage wedges in it. Drizzle the wedges with the olive oil, lemon juice, and soy sauce and season lightly with pepper. Sprinkle the bacon bits over the wedges and cover the skillet loosely with aluminum foil.

4 Place the skillet on the grill, cover the grill, and roast the cabbage until tender, about 30 minutes.

BLT PASTA SALAD

SERVES 4

PREP TIME: 20 minutes
COOK TIME: 31 minutes

10 ounces (280 g) rotini pasta

One 14-ounce (375 g) package bacon, chopped

2 large tomatoes, cut into 1-inch (2.5 cm) chunks

1 tablespoon (4 g) chopped fresh oregano

1 teaspoon minced garlic

Salt and freshly ground black pepper

⅓ cup (80 ml) mayonnaise

⅓ cup (80 ml) sour cream

2 scallions, green part only, chopped

4 cups (140 g) chopped romaine hearts

ALL RIGHT. THIS ONE'S FROM THE KITCHEN, not the grill. But I have found that this salad is such a perfect complement to grilled main courses that I include it here. Or make a big batch and call *this* the main course.

1 Cook the pasta in a large pot of salted boiling water according to the package instructions, about 10 minutes. Drain the pasta, transfer to a large bowl, and set aside.

2 While the pasta is cooking, place a large skillet over medium-high heat and cook the bacon until crisp, about 7 minutes. Transfer the bacon with a slotted spoon to a paper towel–lined plate and discard all but 2 tablespoons (30 ml) of the bacon fat from the skillet.

3 Add the tomatoes, oregano, and garlic to the skillet and stir until warmed through, about 4 minutes. Season the tomato mixture with salt and pepper and add it to the pasta.

4 Add the cooked bacon, mayonnaise, sour cream, and scallions to the pasta; toss to combine. Add the lettuce, tossing to coat the leaves and serve at room temperature.

Smoked
MASHED POTATOES

SERVES 4

PREP TIME: *15 minutes*
COOK TIME: *1 hour*

2 ½ pounds (1,140 g) russet potatoes, peeled and cut into 1-inch (2.5 cm) chunks
½ cup (112 g) unsalted butter, plus extra for topping
½ cup (120 ml) milk
¼ cup (60 ml) sour cream
½ teaspoon salt
¼ teaspoon freshly ground black pepper
½ cup (50 g) grated Parmesan cheese

THE SAME POROUS, AIRY TEXTURE of mashed potatoes that makes them absorb gravy or even sour cream so well also means they will soak up the flavor of wood smoke incredibly well. You won't be sorry you gave this one a try.

1 Preheat the smoker to 350°F (180°C).

2 Place the potatoes in a large saucepan with enough cold water to cover them by 2 inches (5 cm). Bring to a boil over high heat and cook the potatoes until fork-tender, about 15 minutes.

3 Drain the water and use a potato masher to mash the potatoes until no large lumps remain.

4 Add the butter, milk, and sour cream and mash until the desired consistency is reached. Stir in the salt and pepper and adjust the seasonings.

5 Coat a 9-inch (23 cm) cast-iron skillet or grill-safe baking dish with nonstick cooking spray. Spoon the potatoes into the skillet, spreading them evenly. Use a fork to rough up the surface of the potatoes, sprinkle on the Parmesan cheese, and drop small bits of butter all over the surface.

6 Place the mashed potatoes on the grill and smoke for 45 minutes, until golden and piping hot. Serve.

Smoked CREAM CHEESE

MAKES 2 CUPS (480 G)

PREP TIME: *10 minutes*
COOK TIME: *2 hours*

One 8-ounce (227 g) block plain
   cream cheese, chilled
3 tablespoons (18 g) Level Up B Rub
   or your favorite dry rub
Crackers, tortillas, crostini, cut
   veggies, for serving

IT'S NOT A COMPLEX RECIPE, but believe me when I say that this spread is a game-changer. Whether on a bagel, bread, or crackers, this subtly smoky cream cheese adds a whole new dimension of flavor and is a rich indulgence your friends and family will love. You might never go back to plain cream cheese.

1 Preheat the smoker to 225°F (107°C).

2 Score the top of the cream cheese block with a sharp knife into a crosshatch pattern. Sprinkle the seasoning all over the top and sides of the block, and pat it down with the back of a spoons so it sticks.

3 Transfer the cheese to a disposable aluminum bread pan, place it in the smoker with a pan of water, and smoke for about 2 hours. When the cheese puffs up and pulls away from the edges of the pan, it's ready!

4 Serve with your favorite dippers.

Smoked
BACON-WRAPPED ONION RINGS

SERVES 4

PREP TIME: 25 minutes
COOK TIME: 1 ½ hours

3 Vidalia or other sweet onions, cut into ½-inch (1.3 cm) slices and separated into rings
¼ cup (60 ml) sriracha or barbecue sauce
1 pound (455 g) bacon
Dipping sauce, such as mayonnaise, hot sauce, or honey mustard

SOMETIMES I MAKE THESE RINGS HOT AND SPICY, with a sriracha coating and an Asian chili sauce for dipping. At other times I make them Southern style, with a barbecue sauce coating and mayo for dipping. You can try one of those approaches, or you can play around with your own ideas.

1 Preheat the smoker or grill to 300°F (150°C).

2 Separate the larger rings from the smaller ones; you want the same number of rings as bacon slices. Reserve any extras for another recipe.

3 Brush the onion rings with the sriracha and wrap a piece of bacon around each ring through the center so that the onion is completely covered. Secure the bacon with a skewer or toothpick and place the wrapped onion rings on a baking sheet.

4 Place the rings in the smoker (or leave them on the baking sheet) and smoke until the bacon is crispy and the onion is tender, turning halfway through, 1 ½ hours.

5 Remove the skewers and serve the smoked rings with your sauce of choice.

CHAPTER

Six

SAUCES & MARINADES
FOR THE GRILL
AND SMOKER

Chicken
MARINADE

MAKES ABOUT ²/₃ CUP (160 ML)

PREP TIME: 5 minutes

⅓ cup (80 ml) olive oil
3 tablespoons (12 g) finely chopped fresh parsley
2 tablespoons (12 g) paprika
4 cloves garlic, minced
1 ¼ teaspoons salt
½ teaspoon freshly ground black pepper

THIS IS AN ALL-PURPOSE CHICKEN MARINADE for grilling or smoking. You can add other fresh herbs aside from parsley, but start with only 1 tablespoon of each. Other herbs have a stronger, more concentrated flavor than parsley. Marinate the chicken for at least 30 minutes to get the full benefit of the marinade.

1 In a medium bowl or resealable plastic bag, mix the olive oil, parsley, paprika, garlic, salt, and pepper until thoroughly combined. Use immediately.

Rosemary Red Wine
STEAK
MARINADE

MAKES ABOUT ¹/₃ CUP (80 ML)

PREP TIME: 5 minutes

3 tablespoons (45 ml) olive oil
2 tablespoons (30 ml) red wine
1 tablespoon (2 g) dried rosemary
2 cloves garlic, minced
½ teaspoon salt
¼ teaspoon freshly ground black pepper

IF YOU DECIDE TO USE FRESH ROSEMARY in this marinade, remember that a little bit goes a long way. One teaspoon should be enough for up to 2 pounds (910 g) of steak.

1 In a small bowl or resealable plastic bag, mix the oil, wine, rosemary, garlic, salt, and pepper until well combined. Use immediately.

Burger
SAUCE

MAKES ABOUT 1 ½ CUPS (360 ML)

PREP TIME: *5 minutes*

1 cup (240 ml) mayonnaise
½ cup (120 ml) ketchup
1 tablespoon (15 ml) pickle juice
1 teaspoon yellow mustard
1 teaspoon Worcestershire sauce
1 teaspoon chili powder
Salt and freshly ground black pepper

SORRY, I WILL NOT LISTEN TO ANYONE who thinks mayo does not belong on a burger. Stirred into this sauce with seven other ingredients, it adds extra richness and earthiness.

1 In a medium bowl, whisk together the mayonnaise, ketchup, pickle juice, mustard, Worcestershire sauce, and chili powder until well combined. Season with salt and pepper.

2 Refrigerate the sauce in an airtight container for up to 10 days.

Pork Chops
MARINADE

MAKES ABOUT ¾ CUP (180 ML)

PREP TIME: *5 minutes*

¼ cup (60 ml) olive oil
3 tablespoons (45 ml) low-sodium soy sauce
2 tablespoons (25 g) packed brown sugar
1 tablespoon (15 ml) Dijon or grainy mustard
3 cloves garlic, minced
¼ teaspoon freshly ground black pepper

MORE THAN ANY OTHER GRILLED MEAT, pork is complemented by a marinade that has both sweet and sour accents, as here.

1 In a small bowl, mix the oil, soy sauce, brown sugar, Dijon mustard, garlic, and pepper until well combined. Use immediately.

Jamaican
JERK MARINADE

MAKES ABOUT 1 CUP (240 ML)

PREP TIME: 10 minutes

½ small onion, roughly chopped
1 habanero pepper, seeded and stemmed
2 cloves garlic
2 tablespoons (30 ml) freshly squeezed lime juice
2 tablespoons (30 ml) coconut aminos
1 tablespoon (6 g) jerk seasoning mix

A LOT OF PEOPLE GO OUT to restaurants for jerk, but not many—Jamaicans excepted—cook it at home. It's really pretty easy, once you toss together this assertive marinade. Use it on any protein, from beef and pork to seafood and chicken.

1 Place the onion, habanero pepper, garlic, lime juice, coconut aminos, and jerk seasoning in a blender and pulse until mostly smooth. Use immediately.

Garlic-Lemon
BUTTER SAUCE

MAKES ABOUT ½ CUP (120 ML)

PREP TIME: 5 minutes
COOK TIME: 2 minutes

½ cup (112 g) unsalted butter
4 or 5 cloves garlic, minced
1 tablespoon (4 g) roughly chopped fresh parsley
2 teaspoons lemon zest
¼ teaspoon kosher salt

WHEN YOU'RE GRILLING FISH OR SEAFOOD, take a step up from simple squeezed lemon with this easy-to-make alternative.

1 In a small saucepan over medium-low heat, gently melt the butter. Stir in the garlic, parsley, lemon zest, and salt. Simmer for 1 to 2 minutes and remove the saucepan from the heat.

2 Use immediately. If the butter starts to solidify as it cools, reheat over low heat until it melts again.

Remoulade SAUCE

MAKES ABOUT 1 CUP (240 ML)

PREP TIME: 5 minutes

⅔ cup (160 ml) mayonnaise
¼ cup (60 ml) whole-grain mustard
2 tablespoons (30 g) prepared horseradish
1 tablespoon (15 ml) ketchup
2 teaspoons freshly squeezed lemon juice
2 teaspoons dried parsley
2 teaspoons dried chives
2 teaspoons Creole seasoning
1 teaspoon minced garlic
1 teaspoon Worcestershire sauce
½ teaspoon sugar

THE CAJUN AND CREOLE GRILLING traditions of Louisiana are a treasure. This is their signature sauce, and it comes together in no time.

1 In a small bowl or large measuring cup, whisk together the mayonnaise, mustard, horseradish, ketchup, lemon juice, parsley, chives, Creole seasoning, garlic, Worcestershire sauce, and sugar until well combined.

2 Serve immediately or, for enhanced flavor, cover and refrigerate the sauce for 30 minutes to 1 hour before serving.

Spicy AIOLI SAUCE

MAKES ABOUT 1 CUP (240 ML)

PREP TIME: 5 minutes

1 cup (240 ml) mayonnaise
2 cloves garlic, minced
1 tablespoon (15 ml) freshly squeezed lemon juice
1 teaspoon cayenne pepper
¼ teaspoon salt
¼ teaspoon freshly ground black pepper

I SERVE THIS AIOLI WITH any chicken or fish from the grill or smoker when there is not already a richly flavored sauce involved.

1 In a medium bowl, whisk together the mayonnaise, garlic, lemon juice, cayenne, salt, and pepper until smooth.

2 For best results, cover and refrigerate the sauce for 30 minutes to let the flavors meld.

DIY RANCH DRESSING

MAKES ABOUT ½ CUP (120 ML)

PREP TIME: *5 minutes*

3 tablespoons (45 ml) buttermilk
2 tablespoons (30 ml) mayonnaise
2 tablespoons (30 ml) sour cream
1 teaspoon dried minced onion
1 teaspoon dried parsley flakes
½ teaspoon dried chives
¼ teaspoon garlic powder
¼ teaspoon onion powder
¼ teaspoon dried dill
Sea salt and freshly ground black pepper

FOR SALADS, AS A SANDWICH SPREAD, or as a dip for grilled meats, a good homemade ranch is about as useful a thing as you could have in your kitchen.

1 In a small bowl, whisk together the buttermilk, mayonnaise, and sour cream until smooth.

2 Add the dried minced onion, parsley, chives, garlic powder, onion powder, and dill and whisk to combine. Season with salt and pepper to taste.

3 Use immediately or, for the most flavorful result, cover and refrigerate the dressing for 1 hour before serving.

> ***PRO TIP:*** For a thinner consistency, add more buttermilk, 1 teaspoon at a time, until you reach your desired thickness.

CHAPTER

Seven

DESSERTS
& SWEET TREATS

Brown Sugar
GRILLED PINEAPPLE

SERVES 4

PREP TIME: 10 minutes
COOK TIME: 10 minutes

⅓ cup (65 g) packed brown sugar

¼ cup (56 g) unsalted butter, melted

½ teaspoon ground cinnamon

Pinch of salt

1 pineapple, peeled, cored, and cut into ½-inch (1.3 cm) slices

I'LL PUT ANY FRUIT ON THE GRILL, but the first one I'll drape over the hot grates is sliced pineapple. Grilled pineapple is pretty good straight up and unadorned, but this simple brown sugar and cinnamon glaze makes it a whole lot better. Kids coming over? Serve this. Trust me.

1 Preheat the grill to medium, about 350°F (180°C). Coat the grates with nonstick cooking spray.

2 In a small bowl, whisk together the brown sugar, butter, cinnamon, and salt until smooth. Lightly brush the pineapple slices with the mixture.

3 Place the rings, sauce-side down, on the grill. Brush the tops with the mixture.

4 Grill the pineapple, turning and brushing with the brown sugar mixture, until the fruit is lightly caramelized and tender, about 10 minutes total.

Pineapples FOSTER

SERVES 6 TO 8

PREP TIME: *10 minutes, plus marinating time*
COOK TIME: *12 minutes*

½ cup (120 ml) dark rum
1 tablespoon (15 ml) maple syrup
½ cup (100 g) packed brown sugar
¼ teaspoon grated nutmeg
1 teaspoon ground cinnamon, plus more for garnish
1 pineapple, peeled, cored, and cut into 6 to 8 thick rings
Vanilla ice cream, for serving

THIS ONE IS A TREAT SPECIFICALLY FOR YOU PARENTS out there! This pineapples Foster is so fine, with the delicious rum paired with the cinnamon and brown sugar mixture topped with vanilla ice cream, it'll be a hit with all the adults.

1 In a small bowl, stir or whisk together the rum, maple syrup, brown sugar, nutmeg, and cinnamon. Spread out the pineapple rings in a glass dish. Pour the rum mixture over the pineapples, flipping the rings over once so they are well coated. Soak the rings for 20 minutes or more.

2 Drain the extra rum sauce from the dish and put it in a saucepan. Bring the sauce to a medium-low simmer over medium heat and simmer for about 8 minutes, until reduced by half. Keep warm over low heat as you do the next step.

3 Heat a grill pan or sauté pan over medium-high heat and coat lightly with nonstick cooking spray. Add the pineapple slices and cook them for about 2 minutes on each side until they are browned and marked with grill marks. Work in batches if your grill pan is not large enough for all the rings.

4 Place each ring on a plate. Place a scoop of ice cream on top of the center of each ring. Pour the warm rum sauce over the ice cream and serve immediately.

Foil-Pack Grilled BANANA BOATS

SERVES 2

PREP TIME: *10 minutes*
COOK TIME: *10 minutes*

2 large unpeeled ripe bananas, cut lengthwise through the skin about halfway through
¼ cup (25 g) mini marshmallows
¼ cup (45 g) dark chocolate chips
2 graham crackers, broken into pieces

HERE IS MY BACKYARD VERSION OF this well-known campfire recipe, itself a spin on the s'mores concept.

1 Preheat the grill to medium heat, about 350°F (180°C). Turn off one side of the grill.

2 Open the bananas up to create a pocket. Evenly divide the mini marshmallows, chocolate chips, and graham crackers between the bananas, pressing the ingredients as deep as possible into the entire length of the banana.

3 Create two double layers of 12-inch (30.5 cm) square pieces of foil and place a banana in the center of each. Crimp the foil around the banana to form a boat, open at the top.

4 Place the bananas on the unlit side of the grill, close the lid, and cook until the fillings are gooey and the bananas heated through, about 10 minutes. Serve warm.

Grilled
LEMON POUND CAKE WITH PEACHES

SERVES 8

PREP TIME: *15 minutes*
COOK TIME: *1 hour and 5 minutes*

¾ cup (168 g) unsalted butter, plus more for the pan

1 ¾ cups (375 g) sugar

4 large eggs

2 teaspoons (10 ml) pure vanilla extract

2 teaspoons lemon zest

2 ½ cups (300 g) all-purpose flour, sifted, plus more for the pan

¾ teaspoon baking soda

¾ cup (180 ml) sour cream

4 large peaches, cut into eighths

Whipped cream, for serving

UNLIKE MOST CAKES, POUND CAKE HOLDS ITS SHAPE on the grill and is unlikely to break up and fall through the grates. Of course, you are welcome to buy a premade pound cake and start this recipe at step 6. It'll still be good. But nothing beats the taste of a freshly baked pound cake toasted on the grill.

1 Preheat the oven to 350°F (180°C). Lightly grease and flour a 9 by 5-inch (23 by 12.5 cm) loaf pan and set it aside.

2 In a large bowl with a mixer, cream the butter and sugar until light and fluffy, about 5 minutes. Beat in the eggs one at a time, scraping down the sides of the bowl at least twice with a spatula. Beat in the vanilla and lemon zest.

3 In a medium bowl, sift together the flour and baking soda. Fold the flour mixture and sour cream, alternating four times, into the butter mixture until well combined.

4 Spoon the batter into the prepared loaf pan and bake until a toothpick inserted in the center comes out clean, about 1 hour.

5 Let the pound cake cool in the pan for 10 minutes, then turn it out onto a wire rack and let cool completely.

6 Preheat the grill to medium heat, about 350°F (180°C). Lightly coat the grates with nonstick cooking spray.

7 Cut the pound cake into 8 slices using a serrated knife. Grill the cake, turning once, until lightly toasted, about 2 minutes total. Transfer the cake to plates.

8 Coat the grates again with nonstick cooking spray and grill the peach slices until lightly charred and tender, about 3 minutes.

9 Top each slice with whipped cream and peaches and serve.

Grilled
BERRY CRUMBLE

SERVES 6

PREP TIME: 15 minutes
COOK TIME: 35 minutes

2 cups (300 g) mixed berries, such
    as blackberries, blueberries, and
    raspberries
½ cup (100 g) granulated sugar
Juice and zest of 1 lemon
1 teaspoon pure vanilla extract
¼ teaspoon ground ginger
⅛ teaspoon salt
1 cup (120 g) all-purpose flour
½ cup (40 g) rolled oats
½ cup (112 g) unsalted butter,
    melted
¼ cup (50 g) packed brown sugar
½ teaspoon ground cinnamon
Ice cream, for serving

EVEN WITH A SKILLET BETWEEN THE CRUMBLE and the grill grate, you will still get a distinctly outdoorsy flavor when you make this crumble. That's especially true if you spring for some natural-hardwood charcoal, which is more aromatic than charcoal briquettes.

1 Preheat the grill to medium heat, about 350°F (180°C).

2 In a 10-inch (25 cm) cast-iron skillet, combine the fruit, granulated sugar, lemon juice, lemon zest, vanilla, ginger, and salt; set aside.

3 In a medium bowl, mix together the flour, oats, butter, brown sugar, and cinnamon until combined and crumbly. Spread the crumble mixture over the fruit evenly.

4 Place the skillet on the grill, close the lid, and cook the crumble until the filling is bubbly and thickened and the topping is golden, about 35 minutes.

5 Let the crumble cool for 10 minutes and serve with a scoop of your favorite ice cream.

Bloomin' GRILLED APPLES

SERVES 2

PREP TIME: *15 minutes*
COOK TIME: *30 minutes*

1 tablespoon (14 g) unsalted
　　butter, melted
1 tablespoon (12 g) packed
　　brown sugar
¼ teaspoon ground cinnamon
Pinch of ground nutmeg
2 medium apples
¼ cup (60 ml) caramel sauce
2 tablespoons (16 g) chopped
　　pecans
2 scoops vanilla ice cream,
　　for serving

Y'ALL HAVE HEARD OF BLOOMING ONIONS (which can also be grilled; see page 147), but this blooming apple is a showstopper. And a perfect dessert to end everyone's night.

1　Preheat the grill to medium heat, about 350°F (180°C).

2　In a small bowl, mix together the butter, brown sugar, cinnamon, and nutmeg until combined.

3　Cut off the top of the apples and scoop out the core with a spoon or melon baller. Flip the apples over and with a sharp paring knife make ¼-inch (6 mm) cuts all the way around the apple.

4　Place each apple in the center of a piece of foil large enough to wrap around the apple. Spread the brown sugar mixture on the apples and pour 2 tablespoons (30 ml) of the caramel sauce over the apple. Sprinkle each with the pecans. Wrap the apples in the foil, creating a sealed packet.

5　Place the apples on the grill, close the lid, and grill for 30 minutes, or until tender.

6　Open the packets and transfer the apples to plates, pouring any sauce left in the packet over them. Serve with ice cream.

Lemon COCONUT BARS

MAKES 16 BARS

PREP TIME: 15 minutes, plus chilling time
COOK TIME: 15 minutes

For the Crust
2 cups (240 g) all-purpose flour
1 cup (225 g) unsalted butter, at room temperature
½ cup (100 g) sugar
Pinch of salt

For the Lemon Topping
One 14-ounce (396 g) can condensed milk
Juice of 3 lemons
Zest of 1 lemon
1 cup (80 g) shredded unsweetened coconut
2 tablespoons (28 g) unsalted butter, melted

INDULGE ME IN AN OFF-THE-GRILL RECIPE, one I often serve at the end of a grilled dinner. The lemon and coconut speak of warm summer nights, the best time to grill. And—see the end of step 4—you can actually add some grill marks and some toasty grilled flavor by reheating the chilled bars on the grill before serving them.

1 Preheat the oven to 350°F (180°C).

2 To make the crust, in a medium bowl, mix together the flour, butter, sugar, and salt until well combined; press the crust mixture into the bottom of an ungreased 9 by 13-inch (23 by 33 cm) baking pan. Bake the crust until firm and golden, about 15 minutes. Set aside to let cool for 10 minutes.

3 To make the lemon topping, in a medium bowl, whisk together the condensed milk, lemon juice, lemon zest, coconut, and melted butter until well blended. Spread the lemon mixture on the crust and put the baking dish in the refrigerator. Chill for at least 12 hours.

4 When ready to serve, cut into sixteen bars. Serve chilled, at room temperature, or for a special treat, put the bars gently on a hot grill, heat them for 4 or 5 minutes, then remove them, let them cool a little, and serve warm. The bars will keep in the refrigerator for up to 1 week.

Acknowledgments

Alright, y'all, let's take a moment here. Creating my YouTube channel, *Smokin' & Grillin with AB*, and seeing it come to life in my very own cookbook has been one heck of a ride, and let me tell you, it's been all about teamwork!

First things first, I gotta give a massive shoutout to my incredible better half, Kalmele. Your unwavering support and endless love have been the fuel to my fire through this entire journey. Each page of this cookbook carries a piece of your belief in me. Thank you for being my rock; I appreciate and adore you more than words can say.

Now, let's talk about the real MVPs of this whole gig, my partners in crime, Neyda Orozco and Mitzi Olmos. These ladies aren't just assistants; they're the heartbeat of this show, the secret ingredients to our success.

Mitzi, from the early days of helping put together our first cookbook to now taking the reins as our editor, your talent, precision, and knack for creativity have taken our content to the next level. You bring that sizzle that makes every episode pop with flavor. Thank you for turning our recipes into flavorful masterpieces that keep our audience coming back for more.

And Neyda, my right-hand woman; the magician behind the scenes. Your dedication and organizational skills? Absolutely unparalleled. You're the one making sure the gears keep turning, turning my crazy ideas into reality, managing schedules like a pro, and keeping our ship sailing smoothly. You're the secret sauce that makes this whole recipe work, and I couldn't do it without you.

Big love and gratitude to the rest of the amazing team behind the scenes. Mitzi, Neyda, and the gang, your hard work and dedication are the backbone of our success. I'm beyond grateful to have such a talented and dedicated squad.

To all you awesome supporters, viewers, and friends, your enthusiasm and encouragement have been the wind beneath our wings. Your engagement, feedback, and love for our culinary adventures keep us fired up and ready to bring more to the table.

And last, but not least, major thanks to the incredible team at Quarto. Your expertise and dedication in bringing *Smokin' and Grillin' with Aaron Brown* to life has been nothing short of amazing. Your contribution has been vital to our success, and I'm truly grateful for your support.

If I missed anyone, please know your part in this journey is treasured. With *Smokin' and Grillin' with Aaron Brown*, I'm humbled and amped up for what's coming next. Thank you all for being a part of this awesome ride! Let's keep grillin' and smokin' together!

About the Author

AARON BROWN, who goes by the moniker "AB," is a native of south Los Angeles who started his YouTube channel, focused on his parents' and grandparents' traditional grilling and smoking recipes, in 2017, and who quickly grew into one of the most popular food personalities on the entire platform—and across the entire internet. He is also the creator of the "AB Grill Master Series" of sauces and spice rubs for outdoor cooking; and the owner of the Southern Que food truck in Las Vegas, which opened as a brick-and-mortar restaurant in 2023. He lives with his family in Los Angeles and Las Vegas.

Index

Note: Page references in *italics* indicate photographs.